NARRATIVES OF DECONSTRUCTION:
A POSTCOLONIAL STUDY OF SELECT DALIT NOVELS

NARRATIVES OF DECONSTRUCTION:

A POSTCOLONIAL STUDY OF SELECT DALIT NOVELS

U. S. SARANYA

KALPAZ

First Published, 2018

Published by

Kalpaz Publications
C-30, Satyawati Nagar,
Delhi – 110052
E-mail: kalpaz@hotmail.com
Ph.: 9212142040

Printed at: G. Print Process, Delhi

Cataloging in Publication Data—DK
Courtesy: D.K. Agencies (P) Ltd. <docinfo@dkagencies.com>

Saranya, U. S., author.
Narratives of deconstruction : a postcolonial study of select dalit novels / by U.S. Saranya.
pages cm
ISBN 9789386397218 (HB)

1. Indic fiction—Dalit authors—History and criticism. 2. Indic fiction—20th century—History and criticism. 3. Indic fiction—21st century—History and criticism. 4. Dalits in literature. 5. Discrimination in literature. I. Title.

LCC PR9492.5.D35S27 2017 | DDC 891.4 23

Dedicated to My Parents

Mr G. Sadhasivam

and

Mrs S. UmaRani

With Love and Gratitude Forever

Contents

Abstract

The objective of the present study is to introduce and explain the major components of the select Dalit novels in the light of Postcolonial theory. The study is the result of the genuine and bonafide research work done by me. The chapterisation of the thesis entitled "Narratives of Deconstruction: A Postcolonial Study of Select Dalit Novels" is as follows. The introductory chapter offers the meaning and scope of Dalit literature in the light of 'postcolonial theory'. The chapter also deals with how the Dalit literature as a form, from its simplest beginning has now grown into a special and unique form of literature that aims at protesting for the civil rights, especially of the marginalised sections of the country including tribes and minorities. The chapter also tries to re-locate the significance of the philosophical movements that paved the way for the emergence of Dalit literature as an alternative cultural and civil rights movement in India. Chapter–2 offers the thematic concerns and dynamics of the Dalit novel. It also tries to locate the form, style and purpose of Dalit fiction and how the Dalit novel, of recent times, became an instrumental in depicting the true lifestyle of the Dalits through certain imaginary characters. Chapter–3 offers how the caste and religious hegemony by the elites made the marginalised sections of the country feel themselves alienated and excluded from the mainstream society. Chapter–4 argues how the Dalit and other marginalised women are ignored and excluded in all aspects of life. It deals with how the Dalit women have been viewed as mere objects and further exploited. Chapter-5 deals with the findings of my research work.

Foreword

The disciplines of social sciences and humanities have undergone a massive change since the advent of Dalit Studies, more or so during the last three decades. The arrival of Mandal Commission in the early nineties opened the hitherto closed debate of social exclusion on the one hand and exposed the reality of existing caste discrimination on the other. In the wake of these 'disturbing' advancements, Dalit studies as an academic discipline not only democratized the existing intellectual space but also heralded a new set of scholarly inquiries, hitherto neglected and set aside. U. S. Saranya's work *"Narratives of Deconstruction: A Postcolonial Study of Select Dalit Novels*" is yet another contribution in the ever growing discourse on Dalit Studies.

Having noted the contribution of different literary genres in the rise of institutional form of Dalit Studies, Saranya concentrates on the genre of novel to produce her conversation and engagement with the available dalit literary discourse. She critically explores the issues of caste inequality, marginalisation, alienation, humiliation and varied dalit experiences across languages so as to bring out an authentic depiction of dalit life narratives. However, in the process of this comparative analysis, she also manages to expose the breaks and continuities of dalit life worlds in different Indian contexts. The novels for study are meticulously selected so as to accommodate the gendered and regional variations as well. Through her painstaking analysis, the researcher introduces literary experiences into the fold of social and literary theory.

Saranya's work may be considered as an important contribution to the cause of Dalit novel for she foregrounds it as an important vehicle that unveils the deep-rooted biasness of dominant epistemologies. By depositing it as an important offshoot of postcolonial scholarship, which in itself a contentious and provoking statement, the researcher, nevertheless, argues for Dalit novel's capability to further rally the dalit cause.

Through her study, the researcher covers new grounds especially by formulating Dalit subjects as active harbingers of social change. A thesis that traces its roots in the study of marginality, Saranya's work should be consulted by those interested in caste, caste discrimination and social exclusion in general and the genre of Dalit novel in particular.

Varanasi, India

Umesh Kumar, PhD
Assistant Professor
Department of English
Banaras Hindu University

Preface

This book Narratives of Deconstruction: A Postcolonial Study of Select Dalit Fiction is my research. Being thematic in nature, the book is divided into five chapters. The main objective of the book is to bring out the common issues in the select Dalit realistic narratives. Instead of going for a mere textual analysis, I focused on the in-depth analysis of each novel taking the thematic issues into consideration. The text deals with the life aspects of Dalit communities. Dalit literature as a form, from its simplest beginning has now grown into a special and unique form of literature that aims at protesting for the civil rights, especially of the marginalised sections of the country including tribes and minorities. Dalit Novels among the other literary forms remains a successful genre in representing the issues of Dalit culture and movements in Dalit idiom. It is through Dalit Novels, the writers express their sufferings, sorrows and victimisation due to the oppressive culture of caste Hindus.The Dalit novel makes the reader understand that insecure childhood, ever dependence for the assistance of the Government, Socio-cultural oppression, gender dominance, exploitation in paying the daily wages, sexual harassment at the workplaces and physical attacks, police cases and political influence are the day to day experiences of the Dalits. Through their memories, the Dalits reconstruct their broken and long silenced history and demonstrate their rights and identity duly reconstituting themselves with the rest of Dalit communities. The Dalit novel is of rich experiences of the Dalits and paved the way for the formation of their collective consciousness rightly identifying themselves to fight against the Caste and Gender hierarchy.

Acknowledgement

Most importantly, I express my earnest sense of gratitude to my parents G Sadhasivam and S Umarani whose vision made me realise the true value of education.

I would like to thank Dr G Vishwanathan, Chancellor VIT University, the Vice Presidents, Vice Chancellor and Pro-vice Chancellor for their support and guidance. I am grateful to Dr G Buvaneswari, Dean Academic Research, Dr Revathi, Dean, SSL and Dr V. Anitha Devi, Head of the Department of English for their constant encouragement.

I would like to express my deepest gratitude to my research supervisor, Dr Siva Nagaiah Bolleddu for his authentic guidance and constant support throughout my Ph.D research under his able supervision. I would like to offer my sincere thanks to the D C members Professor K. Ratna Shiela Mani, Dr K. V. Raghupathi (external members) and Dr R L N Raju (internal member) for providing necessary feedback and encouraging comments which helped to pursue my research effectively.

I offer thanks to all my scholar friends for their constant support and encouragement. I also offer thank to the editors and publishers for publishing my research articles in their reputed journals.

I also express thanks to the librarians and the staff of VIT, HCU and EFLU, Hyderabad, Samanthara Dalit Book Centre, Hyderabad for providing necessary resources and materials.

Place : Vellore

Date : **U.S. Saranya**

Abbreviations

H	-	Hindu
SC	-	The Stepchild
TW	-	The Taming of Women
UG	-	Untouchable God
US	-	Untouchable Spring
VV	-	Vanmam-Vendetta

Chapter - 1

Dalit Literature: Views and Reviews

In this chapter, I tried to look into various aspects that directly and indirectly the Dalit literature is influenced or confluenced by and also the need for studying Dalit literature in the light of postcolonial theory. The chapter aims at studying the emergence of Dalit literature as an alternative discourse in representing the ever silenced and excluded voices of the Dalits. The proposition of the chapter is also to look into different aspects: socio-political, historical, cultural and linguistic aspects that Dalit literature has succinctly represented so far and how the form and genre of Dalit literature, may be varied in regional dialect but go hand in hand in depicting the neglected promises of the caste-Hindu society which is considered by the Dalits that the caste-Hindu society is religiously conventional and culturally repressive against the Dalits, minorities and women. It also deals with how the Dalit novel, though of recent origin, maintained its own standards and remarkable contributions in narrating the true voice of the Dalits in their own dialect but with an imaginative splutter in content and character. Hence, it is unavoidable discussion of the chapter, to deal with the major forms and genre of the Dalit literature including its most successful forms: poetry and autobiography; Dalit novel and how the Dalit novel is instrumental and perennial to present the issues of caste discrimination, gender bias and construction of Dalit identity both in regional languages and also in English translation.

To define the Dalit literature, Dileep Padgakar writes in *An Anthology of Dalit Literature (Poems)* (1992) that despite its limitations, Dalit literature remains an authentic breakthrough in the otherwise dreary literary scene in the country. Its immense merit is to have effectively rebelled in life as in letters, against the middle-class Hindu who have monopolised cultural expressions. Arjun Dangle in '*Poisoned Bread*'(1994) reveals, Dalit literature came to be used after a stormy discussion organised by the periodical Marathwada in Diwali issue in 1969... The Dalit literature written by the Dalits and that written by others about the Dalits in Marathi be accepted as a separate entity known as 'Dalit literature' and realising its cultural importance, the universities and literary organisations should give it a proper place.

Veena Deo and Eleanor Zelliot in their article "*Dalit literature twenty-five years of Protest or Progress?*" (1994) states Dalit Sahitya, the "literature of the oppressed," emerged on the Indian scene to make a profound difference in the field of Marathi literature, and a few years later, to Kannada and Gujarati, the neighbouring languages, as well. "Dalit" is the name politically conscious ex-Untouchables now use in preference to Untouchable, Harijan, a caste name, or the governmental term Scheduled Castes, since it is more inclusive and implies no fault, no "untouchability" on the part of the Dalits. The literary movement flowered as part of the social and political movement of Dr. B.R. Ambedkar (1891-1956), particularly after the conversion to Buddhism he undertook in the year of his death.

Eleanor Zelliot in her book, "*From Untouchable to Dalit: Essays on the Ambedkar Movement*" (1996) states that Dalit literature, that is, writing which is considered genuine literature rather than folk-protest poetry and "movement" literature, may be said to have begun in the late 1950s... Dalit literary conferences have resulted in what must be called a significant new school of Marathi writing, that of Dalit literature.

Waman Nimbalkar in his book "*Dalit Literature Nature and Role*" (2006) opines about Dalit literature as the transformation from the past Dalit consciousness into present condition is the birth spring or source of Dalit literature. He further adds that the advent of Ambedkar bore two mellifluous fruits which brought about a social revolution in India during the twentieth century they are Dalit literature and Dalit Panthers. In his view, Dalit literature is nothing but the human literature as for the first time he claims that literature about the human was written in a realistic way and Dalit literature is nothing but a medium to express the thoughts of Ambedkar. According to Nimbalkar, being a Dalit and to possess Dalit consciousness are two different things. Literature that is created with Dalit consciousness about Dalit life is Dalit literature.

Nimbalkar (2006) also considers what Sada Karhade puts three different tendencies for Dalit literature they are:

1. The tendency to proclaim knowingly an insurrection, refusal, protest, and anger.
2. The tendency to bring society together by hitting with a whip in anger at untruth, injustice, and pretension.
3. The tendency to destroy Hinduism to brighten the future of the country.

Nimbalkar's *Dalit Literature: Nature and Role (2006)* further offers how the Dalit Sahitya Sammelan which was held in Nagpur in 1976 raises numerous meanings of what the Dalit literature is. To view some of them: Professor Yashwant Manohar says, literature is the literature of victims of class and Varna. This is the literary conflagration of Dr Ambedkar's speech. These are the creative expressions of those neglected hearts and brain whose stomachs and mind have been kept hungry by culture. In the womb of this literature, an embryo of human-centered civilised age is growing with stormy determination. According to Sardar, Dalit literature is being written out of intense, burning experience and consciousness. The doggedness of self-revealing and self-developing new society is reflected at every step in this literature. In his point of view, he states that Dalit literature voices out against racism and casteism dealing with Dalit consciousness with life oriented literature.

Limbale (2007) further states that the mute society found its hero in Babasaheb, and its anguish voice through him. This anguish of Dalits is the progenitor of Dalit literature. It is not the pain of any one person, nor is it of just one day- it is the anguish of many thousand years. Therefore, it is expressed collectively. The anguish of Dalit literature is not that of an individual but of the entire outcaste society.

Limbale (2007) states the true reasons behind the Dalit writing. He states that there has not been a realistic delineation of Dalits in ancient, modern and contemporary Marathi literature. In order to provide a realistic portrait of Dalits, Dalit writers will have to write and Dalit writers have written inspired by the purpose of depicting in literature the authentic experiences of Dalit life. He further states that the experience of Dalit writings as it is not possible to close one's eyes to the experience of the untouchables because it is the experience of thousands of people over thousands of years.

Yaggati Chinna Rao in the forward of the book "*A History of Telugu Dalit Literature*" (2008) states that Dalit literature has evolved in modes of representation characterised by realistic, metaphysical, philosophical, symbolic and imaginative language. Dalit literature inspired by experiences of everyday life, its images and values take precedence over speculation or mere imaginations. Thus, to Dalit writers, narratives are far from being illusionary or unreal as authenticity and liveliness are the hallmarks of Dalit literature Thummapudi Bharati (2008) also has the similar opinion and she states that Dalit literature is deliberately used as a weapon to fight for the human rights of Dalits.... The literature is used as one of the weapons in the struggle.

In an article "*Dalit Autobiographies: Graphs of Pain*" Waman Nimbalkar (2009) states that Dalit literature has acquired momentum since the last fifty years. It started developing and blossoming with genres like poetry, stories, novels, autobiographies and dramas. As compared to poetry, all other genres of literature were being written in less proportion but in a nourishing and thriving manner. Various aspects of life were unfolded one by one gradually because the Dalits in Indian society have remained the most exploited persons of the world for a longer period of time. He further states that the slavery, injustice, inflicted upon him and the atrocities committed for thousands of years were tortuous, terrible and equally contemptible. The Dalits led a benumbed existence like a stone without any sensation due to ignorance, poverty, sycophancy, superstitions and improper customs and traditions. The emotional world of the Dalits was destroyed; his power of imagination and thinking was destroyed. He further states that Dalit literature has breathed a new life in this emotional world. Dalit literature has blossomed to provide expression and meaning to life that was suppressed for so many years. It started spitting fire at the atrocities and injustices inflicted upon Dalit life. It started providing it heroic nature in stories and novels.

According to Sreenivasan, the chief editor of the *Journal of Literature and Aesthetics,(2009)* Since the 1960s with the emergence of the first generation of post-independent educated sections of Dalit youths, there has been a new awakening, an upsurge, an intense awareness, driving them to liberate themselves from the restraints of an age-old, caste-based repressive social order. Dalit literature has sprung from this new five consciousness, this historic urge for liberation. Among other things, it seeks to assert the human rights of the Dalits, to retrieve their lost identity, to dismantle Hindu mythology and to diagnose the social psyche of the dominant class. It is not the expression of "pure feeling" or "poor form". It is the imaginative expression of a deeply subjective response to the actual conditions of living in the benumbing atmosphere of the stratified Indian society, still, considered as literature, it has a pristine, luminous quality. Although it has possible limitations in terms of theme and refinement of techniques, its energy of art and vision possess a transformative power, a potential for the renewal of hope for a more humane and just society. Dalit literature needs to be studied in a larger perspective.

Tarachand Khandekar, (2010) a Dalit writer, opines that literature is for the human beings hence to be written by the human beings. He writes:

> Man is the centrifugal force in the philosophy of Dalit literature. The man is supreme. He is above all Gods, sacred books and science. It is the man who can make and unmake anything. Dalit literature believes that nothing is permanent. Everything is subjected to decay. With every decay, there is a resurgence of the new creation. It, therefore, does not accept the maxim 'Sathyam, Siva, Sundaram.' On the other hand, it proclaims that nothing is true which is not applicable for man's sublime freedom, nothing is good if it's not useful for man's welfare, nothing is beautiful which is not useful for beautification of mankind.

Nagaraj, (2010) one of the Dalit activists and critic, in his book "*The Flamming Feet*" states that Dalit literature, then, is often now the product of a new generation of militant Dalits whose rejection of Hindu society is total… Dalit writing now is essentially a product of the Ambedkarite vision of life. A strong sense of self-respect and dignity informs the new style of writing. A feeling of intensity is the second major quality to be found in Dalit writing.

Arun Prabha Mukherjee (2010) in her introduction to Sharankumar Limbale's novel "*Hindu*" traces the evolution of Dalit literature as "Dalit literature as a term came into being with the first conference of Dalit writers, held on 2nd March 1958 where a resolution was passed to the effect that the cultural importance of Dalit literature should be acknowledged and the literature given due recognition". She further quotes the words of Sharankumar Limbale as a unique feature of Dalit literature is its collective aspects. The experience described in Dalit literature is social, hence it is articulated as collective in character.

Sunny M. Kapikkad (2012) in his article "*The Dalit Presence in Malayalam literature*" traces that

> Dalit presence in Malayalam literature becomes meaningful only when it opens up new vistas of aesthetics. Dalit literary studies which includes anything that is written about Dalits in the purview of Dalit literature parades 'Duravastha', 'Vazhakkula', and 'Kurathi' as Dalit literature. He even adds that Dalit is not only a common term for designating the untouchables. But the word has a history that they refuse to acknowledge. It became part of the socio-political discourse of the turbulent 1960's as an epitome of India's dream of liberation. It carries the weight not only of strife but also of centuries-long philosophical enquiry...Dalit literature burgeoned in the creative engagement that the Indian psyche had with this peculiar formation of history…Dalit literature has been misunderstood as antisavarna propaganda precisely because of the failure to understand the different aesthetic sensibility. He further adds that Dalit literature is a mode of self-expression that history has invented against class and caste values and their aesthetics that bind us in a vice-like grip. As in the case

of any other literature, the life breath of Dalit literature is also its anxieties about human liberty. It advances by making intrepid incursions into language and the value system towards its realisation.

Ravikumar and Azhagarasan in their book "*Oxford Anthology of Tamil Dalit Writing" (2012)* states that the emergence of Dalit literature in languages such as Marathi, Kannada, Telugu, Hindi, Gujarati, Punjabi, and Tamil in recent decades is an important and encouraging sign of our times. Once it launched itself, it spread like forest fire, gaining further momentum during the birth centenary celebrations of Dr. Ambedkar in 1991. Although it belongs to a century we just left behind, the recovery of Dalit history helps us trace the origins of Dalit literature to ancient Buddhist or medieval anti-caste movements... before the birth of the word Dalit there was a recorded history of the untouchables fight against discrimination and literary expression that spoke about it.

Ravi Kumar and Azhagarazan (2012) further add that we normally view 'Dalit literature' as having originated in Marathi in the 1970's. But there is an active century old distinct Dalit history and culture in Tamil Nadu. Following Iyothee Thass, one may now see the possibility of tracing the antiquity of Dalit literature by reclaiming Tiruvalluvar as a Buddhist. Since the non-Hindu and anti-discriminatory contents of present-day Dalit literature show certain parallels with the contents of early secular Tamil literature, we cannot dismiss this interpretation merely as an imaginary claim of Iyothee Thass. He even traces how the Dalit literature in Tamil Nadu had a Marxist ground. He states that "they fail to identify the unique features of Tamil Dalit literature in the light of the Buddhist past, which forms the basis of the Dalit question in Tamil Nadu. While Marxist reduced the interpretation of Dalit literature to an expression of class oppression, Periyarists saw Dalit literature as a branch of non-Brahmin literature. Those who felt disturbed by the Dalits critique of other backward castes started feeling alienated from Dalit literature. They saw Dalit literature as a reaction against the non-Brahmin, non-Dalit castes. Unable to understand this, literary critics began suspecting Dalit literature of having a secret pact with Brahmins. This has led to the following stereotypes: (a) literature foregrounds the voice of the victims, and (b) caste is substituted with class. These stereotypes caused great damage to Dalit literature.

Ravikumar (2012) further putsforth that unlike the anti-Brahminism of non-Brahmins which is firmly located within Hinduism, his anti-Brahmin critique is rooted within the history of a Tamil Buddhism. If there are similarities between the non-Brahmin and Dalits, there are also significant differences. This is the hallmark of Tamil Dalit literature...Contrary to the view that Tamil Dalit literature has reached a state of stagnation, we might now understand that it travels in a different direction. It marches towards the cultural history of Tamils with the strength gained from archival and archaeological.

In the book, "*Steel Nibs are Sprouting*" (2013) the author Satyanarayan in the introduction puts forth the question of B.M. Puttaiah as what is Dalit literature and what is not considered as Dalit literature as One it was proposed that any literature from non-Ambedkarite perspective cannot be considered Dalit writing. In other words, the long tradition of writing about Dalits from a Marxist perspective was rejected as Dalit writing in the 1990's.

Om Prakash (2014) in his research paper, *Dalit literature in India: Some features*", states that Dalit literature is concerned with the emotions and aspirations of the Dalits. It is a particular brand of literature in which a particular community is free to speak its mind in literary works such as poems, short stories, novels, dramas and autobiographies. He further adds that Dalit literature is an expression of anguish and anger. Dalit writing is an expression of anguish and anger of a community (that is, Dalit community). It protests against social injustice, inequality, cruelty and economic exploitation based on caste and class. Poetry seems to be the dominant mode of Dalit voice or expression. Dalit literature symbolises humanitarian cause.

Manoja (2014) in her article of "*Beginning of the Marathi Dalit Literature*" states that it has emerged as very important distinct part of literature. Though Dalit literature is comparatively a contemporary phenomenon inspired on Buddhist ideology, Marxism and Mahar movement, the epoch-making Bhakti movement in Maharashtra protested against the exploitation of the oppressed. She further states that expressions in literature soon gained their importance. Silenced for centuries by prejudices and oppression the writers in the pathways of Ambedkar continued to register their anguish and protest in almost all genres of literature, importantly biographies and autobiographies. She concludes the article as Dalit literature has spawned new literary canons and new aesthetic imagination. It is the signal that Dalit cultures are edging out their lines to carve the new niches. The legacy of ancient wisdom and present intellectual awareness put Dalit writings to reflect them in an effective way.

B.V. Bhosale (2014) in his book, *"Sociology of Dalit Literature"* (2014) traces that the term "Dalit Literature" first appeared in Dalit literary conference in 1958, organised by Maharashtra Dalit Sahitya Sangha. It was the resolution No. 5, passed at the conference mentioned that writing of Dalits and other non-Dalits concerning the Dalits is called Dalit literature.

According to Bhosale (2014), Dalit literature in India, especially Dalit literature in Maharashtra emerged in 1960's and 1970's. It was in the writings of Namdeo Dhasal, Raja Dhale and others who were the founders of Dalit Panthers movement in Maharashtra in 1970's we saw the beginning of writings in Dalit literature. There were two categories of writers who wrote on and about Dalits, one from amongst the Dalits and another non-Dalits, upper caste, writers writing on the issue of caste. In the late nineteenth and early twentieth centuries writers like Rabindranath Tagore in Bangla, Prem Chand in Hindi and Mulk Raj Anand in English were writing on the issue of Untouchability. Later, writers from the Dalits emerged on horizons and took up the cause and started elaborative writing about the sufferings of caste, discrimination, humiliation, exploitation, oppression and how Dalits have experienced the worst of inhumanness. Bhosale (2014) further adds that Dalit literature is the reflection of individual, community, enlightenment and consciousness of self and reality around.

Bhosale (2014) states that Between 1972-1978 there emerged writers from Dalit community in Gujarat, Karnataka, Andhra Pradesh, Odisha, and Tamil Nadu who started writing about the caste exploitations. In his book, "*Sociology of Dalit Literature*" (2014) Bhosale traces the origin of Dalit literature in Different states as in Gujarat he states that Dalit literature is influenced by Marathi Dalit literature. "Panthers" was started by Ramesh Chandra Parmar in1975. Parmar's famous book titled, *Hath Ma Jhadu Mathe Mailu* (1996) gives the heart rendering account of bhangis… In 1980's "Poetry and Prose emerged in Gujarati which was written by Dalits. Some writers like Joseph Macwan, Mohan Parmar, Harish Mangalam, Mangal Rathod, Kisan Sosa are very well acknowledged in the literature circle of Gujarat". Bhosale adds about other states also in his book as in Karnataka the Dalit writing emerged in the early 1970's. D.R. Nagaraj a famous critic made a distinction between two schools of Kannada Literature. Siddaalingaiah and Devanoor Mahadeva were the first generation Dalit writers in Kannada Dalit literature. According to Bhosale in Tamil Nadu, the Dalit writings started in 80's and 90's. Writers like Imayam, Bama, Sivakami are acclaimed writers in Tamil Nadu. In Andhra, writers like Joshua Garran, Mohan Rao, Boya Jangaiah and Akkieni Kutumba Rao have produced notable works in Telugu. In Hindi, autobiographies emerged as the main form of Hindi Dalit literature and produced eminent writers like Omprakash Valmiki, Jai Prakash Kardarm, Mohandas Namishra, Suresh Chandra and Sheoraj. In Punjab, the Dalit writings originated in 80's and 90's. Dalit Sahitya Sabha was formed and first Dalit Sahitya Samelan was held in 1994 and writers like Prem Gorkhi, Kripal Kazak, Attarjee, Bhura Singh, Kaler and many other eminent writers emerged in Punjab. Bhosale says that Dalit literature is the reflection of individual, community enlightenment and consciousness of self and reality around. He further states that Dalit literature has been reflecting on certain aspects of life, society and economy. Sociology has to enrich its content by learning from literature appearing from various subaltern groups at the level of caste, gender and region. Dalit literature is a source of knowledge and therefore a source of primary data, which can sharpen our sociological understanding. Dalit literature has touched the essence of caste and gender.

According to Panchancan Dalai (2014) states that Dalit literature is aimed at questioning, rejecting and revolting against the Brahminical order or Hindu code of civilisation… it aims at decoding the

Brahminical rituals, culture, texts and literature that were/ are instrumental in exercising their supremacy over the Dalits. He further adds that the subversive act of Dalit literature lies in its attempts to erase the prejudices, male violence, and insidious intentions of Hinduism and Hindu sacred texts and their theory of purity, pollution, sin and salvation. Dalit literature fundamentally questions the theory of Varna or Jati system that facilitated, and still facilitates, Dalits' subordination and segregation for centuries in India…Dalit literature makes a persistent endeavour to deconstruct such order in order to promote a rational and reasonable understanding of humans and human society. Dalit literature embodies this subversive ideology of deconstructing, defining, rewriting, and rejecting the aesthetics of cultured people. Panchanan Dalai (2014) further adds that Dali literature in its characters in not individualistic but collective. Considering pain and anguish as the progenitor of Dalit literature he adds Limbale's opinion also as Considering Dalit writing as a means of human liberation. By doing so, Dalit writers can establish Dalit literature not as propagandist but unique, liberating, collective, and social. The predominance of collective experience or communal memory cannot be ignored or rejected when one looks at it. Dalit writers thus move carefully from a personal plane to a general conscience and in this move they are constantly reminded of their responsibility and 11 commitment to follow Dalits and exploited classes. The predominance of their personal lives and personal experience and the urgency to share them with the larger audience, particularly the Dalits and exploited classes, thus make Dalit literature appear testimony-based and autobiographical.

Raj Kumar (2014) opines that Dalit literature is enriched and beautified by the life-force only. Sincere revolutions and forceful representations go to make it so. Established value has been discarded in Dalit projections as despicably in justifiable, inclined or too narrow in themselves…The so called style, form, construction that is the outward decorum find insignificant attention in Dalit creation. Contrarily, it lays an added emphasis on the intensity of experience and feeling or vital emotion…such a form gains…naturalness and fragrance of its own kind. So it grows and enthuses and injects a new spirit of values to bring about social transformation.

Sasidharan (2015) in his article, "*Key-Text in Hindi Dalit Literature: A Thumbnail Analytical Sketch*" states that Dalit literature is written drawing inspiration from the life of the subjugated, their bitter experiences and their fight for equal rights. It is a body of literature written by a group of people who have been denied all forms of human freedom and were thrown to the dump-yards of Indian society. 'Dalit' does not stand for a caste or a religion; on the contrary, it's a label for a group of people who have been exploited and suppressed for long. When the word Dalit is attached as an adjective to literature, such literature becomes a separate stream of the literature of extreme sensitivity and dedication. Dalit literature depicts people who have been experiencing social inequality, marginalisation, and negligence. Dalit literature takes it birth from the consciousness of being a Dalit. Even in this new millennium, Dalits are still exploited socially, politically, mentally, and economically. When such exploited people became aware of the exploitation, and atrocities committed against them, Dalit literature came into being as a cultural by-product. He further quotes the words of Baburao Bagul, Dalit literature is a literature that fights for humanistic values that stand against all forms of apartheid. Apartheid is nothing but a form of warfare of hatred, competition and rejection. Love, brotherhood, equality, peace, prosperity etc. are the values that stand against colour based discrimination. He further states that Dalit literature is actually the mouthpiece of Dalit movement. From this, it is understood that Dalit literature is not a literature that prioritises imagination; on the contrary, but it is actually a cultural or revolutionary movement.

Anil Suresh (2015) in his research article traces that the distinctiveness of Dalit literature lies in its authentic unity of language and content. In it the disillusionment and disgust of young Dalits, often accompanied by a desire for revenge, come alive. It revives the memory of the pain and suffering of past generations. It confronts centuries of hypocrisy, deceit and violence sustained in the name of tradition.

Shruti Das in her article (2015), "*Intertextual Process in Limable's Towards an Aesthetic of Dalit Literature: History, Controversies and Considerations*" states that Dalit literature is a body of writing by the

Dalits steeped in Dalit consciousness that rejects beauty and pleasure in favour of social values, conditions and life-affirming realism. They reject traditional aesthetics for a new aesthetic, depicting constant struggles to express the all that is non-logical to the hegemonic aesthetics so far.

Shriti Das (2015) further states that Dalit literature aesthetics can only exist in a conflict of dialogism and cannot be prescriptive. There it cannot exist a general concept of beauty or aesthetics and Dalit literature cannot subscribe to the idea that literature privileges pleasure derived from beauty. The rasa would be rewritten as new rasa depicting the taste of pain, anger, rejection, rebellion, problems, struggles, injustices and ill-treatment contained in Dalit literature.

Arvind (2015) further adds that Dalit literature is full of metaphors and imagery of darkness, dirt, filth and violence. The society is caught in the grip of age-old superstition and traditional beliefs that prevent them from undergoing fundamental changes. So Dalit literature has emerged as a revolt against the century's long exploitation and heinous treatment towards the lowest strata of the Indian society and it gives expression of the sufferings, frustration and torture imposed on them and their revolt against this inhuman treatment. Dalit literature can be called the voice of those who were condemned to silence for thousands of years. It expresses the dilemma, pangs, predicament and injustice meted out to Dalits. It portrays the life and struggles of low caste for the dignity, justice and equality. It is also a protest against the established unjust social order. Arvind concludes the article as Dalit literature proved its importance in portraying the stigmatised and hapless conditions of Dalits, upstaging the subjugation of caste oriented society. As literature has always served as a medium in bringing change in socio-political scenario, so Dalit literature does and provides a platform to oppressed people to stand against the social problems like poverty, religious fanaticism and untouchability.

Raj Kumar (2015) further states that Dalit texts travel much greater distance in terms of sharing the author's lived experience, and in the process mobilise opinion against caste exploitation and oppression. Since the main aim of Dalit literature is to bring a social order based on equality, justice and self-respect the act of translation plays an important role furthering these causes.

Anitha (2015) in her article, *"Aesthetics in Dalit Literature"*, brings about Dalit literature as it moves beyond the usual discourses of literary modernity. Dalit literature is powerful medium of expression that keeps Dalit movement sustaining and provides an untiring zeal. Dalit literature – short stories, novels, critical essays, autobiographies, plays etc. provides critical insight to the question of Dalit identity. Anitha (2015) further draws about Dalit literature as a literary expression of political consciousness among Dalits. It primarily narrates first hand experience of community: aiming to make aware multiple oppressions and also trying protest against the domination of the upper castes in Indian society. Writings of Dalit writers such as Namdev Dhasal, Daya Pawar, Prahlad Chandvarkar, Tryambak Sapke, Arjun Dangle, Prakash Jadhav and Shiva Ingole captured the problems, pain and torture faced by and experienced by the community more authentically. Their writings are not only interpreted as a piece of artistic work but more as representatives of that time and situations faced by that community.

Anitha (2015) concludes in her article with her opinion as Dalit literature manifests expression of cardinal values of independence, justice, equality, and fraternity. If depicts real picture of the community, its trauma and its struggle for social change…Thus, Dalit literature is a journey from the main stream to marginal literature from grand narrative to little narrative, from individual identity to group identity and from self-justification to self-affirmation.

Though caste consciousness is the subject matter of Dalit literature, new paradigms for thinking about gender and social differences are emerging out of transformations in social life. Almost all writers express their experiences and concerns and all literary discourses articulate the whole range of emotions-pain, humiliation, resentment, anger, resistance. Such writings have always opened up discursive space for negotiating issues of untouchability and oppression. Dalit literature is the space where a community can prove themselves, assert their self, express their identity and expose the social truth. Most of the literatures produced by Dalit authors are part of their struggle against caste discrimination. Their writings are rooted in their cultural–material world and employ innovative strategies in both form and content, challenging, at the same time enriching existing literature. Any attempt to explore and analyse those literary outpourings, characterised by a kind of new Dalit aesthetic will enable us to re-situate Dalit literature, as literature.

Dalit literature in Maharashtra emerged out of the literary movements which grew out of conversions of Dalits, especially, 'Mahars' to Buddhism. Hence this conversion unlike other conversions is remarkable in literature. Marathi Dalit writings of Dalit as well as non-Dalit writers have Buddhist influences in their works. A large number of Dalits who had to undergo opprobrium of public abuse, having to live without self-respect embraced Buddhism which marked a new era in their lives since it gave them new socio-religious and political identity. Though caste consciousness and social differences are subjects of Dalit writings there are other lots many similarities-issues of gender and the question of human dignity. The subjugation of Dalits by the privileged in the name of religion and tradition is delineated in such writings.

Chintha Syam Sunder (2015) in his article, "*The Meaning of Dalit and its True* Perceptions by Indian Society and Dalit Writers through Translations: An Analytical *Study"* states that in recent times Dalit literature has become a new genre. The writers of Dalit literature have started depiction the tormenting experiences of Dalits exposed to present the contemporary social, political, economic, educational and mental conditions of Dalits before Dalit and non-Dalit readers. A Dalit in India can stand in comparison with a Dalit in Africa or America concerning his/her mutation. The writers of Dalit literature questioned religion and identity throughout their works.

Pavan Mandavkar (2015) in his article, '*Indian Dalit literature quest for identity to social equality*' states that as obvious from the meaning Dalit literature is the writing about and of Dalits or oppressed.

Sajjin Singh and Anjali Srivastava (2016) in their article, '*Dalit literature in India: An Agitation to a Genre*' traces that Dalit literature is based on experience. Most of writers wrote their own experience of life and that is why we find a streak of autobiographical note in their works.

K. Purushotham, Gita and Gogu Shyamala (2016) in their book "*The Oxford Indian Anthology of Telugu Dalit Writing*" draw the opinion of Sivasagar about the non-Dalit writing Dalit life can considered to be Dalit literature or not. For which the answer is: It is meaningless for a man to write on feminism and for a non-Dalit to write about Dalits… A Brahmin, instead of writing about Dalits can serve the Dalit cause by writing how Brahmins ill-treated the Dalits; about the narrow-mindedness of the Brahmin that they are so familiar with; how they subordinated the Dalits etc. In their General introduction in their book they states that Dalit writing are the elements of modernity in social constructs, self-representation in politics, and the post-modernist thrust on celebrating diversity. Dalit writings are, in fact, ahead of post-modernism in representing the question of subordination within diversity. In Dalit writing, there is a transition from humiliation to humanism, from an undesirable past to a cultural present, from agitation to transformation.

The introductory chapter is aimed at offering various definitions expressed by critics and scholars on Dalit literature. The chapter has also highlighted the origin and growth of Dalit literature and how, now, Dalit literature is being recognised as a unique and independent genre of literature succinctly representing the voice of the voiceless in their own dialect. Chapter 2 entitled "Dalit Literature in English and in Translation" offers how Dalit literature in English translation paved the way for reaching the larger world rightly subscribing the similar identities that of native literature especially Native Canadian, Native American and Australian Aboriginal studies. The chapter deals with the theory of translation studies and how the method of historical translation finds its resonance and applicability of rewriting the untouched history of the Dalits in the form of novel.

Chapter - 2

Dalit Literature in English and in Translation

Chapter 2 offers the form and purpose of Dalit novel and how it emerged as a significant genre for depicting the true lifestyle of Dalits through certain imaginary characters. The chapter also offers the key aspects of Dalit novel especially setting, plot, characterisation and thematic concerns which are completely new and different Indian English fiction. The chapter provides a list of Dalit novels available in English and in translation. A synoptical note on the select novel is an integral part of the chapter.

Dalit as a word was used in India only after independence by which the Dalits gained inspiration from the pioneers like Jyothirao Phule, Buddha and Ambedkar. Hinduism as a religion divided man from man and it did not unite them into humanity. The Dalit writers and the writings are real, authentic and lively these are the hallmarks of the Dalit literature. The stories of the Dalits are untold and unheard history and to make the unknown known to the world is the emergence of Dalit literature. Dalit writings put forth the religious oppression, caste-based discrimination.

The writings of Dalit men portray the atrocities of the upper caste men and the writings of women portray the double oppression faced by the upper caste men and the men from their own caste. Various feminist Dalit movements voiced out for brutal patriarchy, sexual violence and gender disparities and to make the Dalit women realise their power to lead an authentic life. Male Dalit writers complain about the humanism of the upper caste and on the other hand, they Discriminate, Torment and Sexually Abuse Their Own Female Clan Without Humanity.

2.1 Emergence of the Marathi Dalit Literature

Only after the advent of the Dalit Panther movement, Dalit literature started to emerge into the mainstream. Ambedkar with the inspiration of Phule awakened the deep slumber of the Dalits to exploit the caste-based issues which prevailed in the society. Eleanor Zelliot (1992) traces that the Dalit Sahitya which means the literature of the oppressed in Maharashtra is unique in the quantity of writing, its variety, its aesthetic consideration, its sense of being a movement, its tie to social action, and in the serious attention it receives as a school within the Marathi literary traditions. Zelliot (1992) even states that from Maharashtra the Dalit writing is slowly spreading to other states as Tamil Nadu, Karnataka, Gujarat, Andhra Pradesh and on one day the literature of oppressed will be an all-India movement.

After the Dalit Panther movement which emerged in Maharashtra in 1972 many genres of writing came into the stream the writers brought out their unexpressed feelings through Poetry, Autobiography, Essays, Novels, Speeches and Short Stories. Arjun Dangle who is the pioneer of Dalit Panther movement compiled various genres of works of the Marathi Dalit writing as *Poisoned Bread: Translation from Modern Marathi Dalit Literature (1994)* Eleanor Zelliot and Mulk Raj Anand produced a book on Poetry entitled as *An Anthology of Dalit Literature* (1992).

The main writers who contributed to Poetry are L.S. Rokade's, *To be or not to be Born,* Tryambak Sapkale's *That Single Arm,* Damodar More's *Reading, Song,* Waman Kardak's *Send my Boy to School,* Bhimsen's *Song*, Keshav Meshram's *In our Colony,* Prakash Kharat *The Sky with its Eyes Closed,* Arjun Kamble's *Yesterday they have Announced,* Yashwant Manohar's *An Ultimatum,* Pralhad Chendwankar's *My Father,* Vaharu Sonawane's *In the Lush Green Jungle,* Jyoti Lamjewar's *Caves,* Narendra Patil's *Exhalation,* Vilas Rashinkar's *No Entry for the New Sun,* Sudhakar, S. Gaikwad's *The Unfed Begging Bowl,* D.S. Dudhlkar's *Wall,* Ashok Chakravathi's

Harvest, Bagwan Sawai's *Two Poems,* Hira Bansode's *Yashodhara,* Suresh Kadam's *To Dear Aana,* Uttam Kolgaokar's *His House,* Dharmaraj Nimsarkar's *Experiment,* Waman Nimbalkar's *Mother,* Bapurao Jagtap's *This Country is Broken,* B.S. Hate's *The Stains of Blood,* Arjun Dangle's *I will Belong to it,* J.V. Pawar's *Birds in Prison,* Namdeo Dhasal's *Hunger,* B. Rangarao's *On a Desolate Night like this,* Baban Chahande's *Labour Pain,* Prakashchandra Karandikar's *Amen,* Bhujang Meshram's *Winds,* Baban Londhe's *Shroud,* Shankar Kharat's *The Death-doomed March,* Meena Gajabhiye's *Light Melted in Darkness,* Arun Kamble's, *Language should I Speak?,* W. Karpur's *which The Search,* Prakash Jadhav's *Under Dadar Bridge,* Manohar Wakode's *It is not Binding on us to undertake this journey,* Bhau Panchbhai's *How?,* Daya Pawar's *Blood Wave,* Sharankumar Limbale's . *White Paper,* Umakant Randhir's *A Poem,* Yusoja's *Mute Existence,* Shiva Ingole's *Ancient Mother Mine,* F.M. Shinde's, *Habit,* Baburao Bagul's *You Who Have Made the Mistake.*

Some Writers who contributed to Autobiography are Shankarroa Kharat's *A Corpse in the well,* Daya Pawar's *Son Eat your Fill, We are Kings,* Shantabai Kamble's *Naja Goes to School and Doesn't,* Kumud Pawde's *The Bone Merchant,* Sharankumar Limbale's *The Bastard,* Dadasaheb More's *The Stragglers,* P.E. Sonkamble's *This too Shall Pass.*

The emerging works in Short stories are Bandhumadhav's *The Poisoned Bread,* Waman Hoval's *The Storeyed House,* Yogiraj Wanghmare's *Explosion,* Arjun Dangle's, *Promotions*, Bhimrao Shirvale's *Livelihood,* Baburao Bagul's *Mother,* Amitabh's *The Cull,* Keshav Meshram's *The Barriers,* Annu Bhau Sathe's *Gold from the Grave,* Avinah Dolas's *The Refugee.*

Some contributed for Essays and Speeches they are Dr Ambedkar's *Speech at Mahad*, Arjun Dangle's *Dalit Literature: Past, Present and Future,* Sharatchandra Muktibodh's *What is Dalit Literature,* Baburao Bagul's *Dalit literature is human literature,* Raosaheb Kasbe's *Some Issues before Dalit literature,* R.G. Jadhav's *Dalit Feelings and Aesthetic Detachment,* Janardan Waghmare's *Black literature and Dalit literature,* M.N.Wankhade's *Friends, the Day of irresponsible Writers is Over.*

All forms of genres other than novel are worked but novel gained its importance only in late twentieth century some novels are Sharankumar Limbale's *Hindu* (2010), *Upalya, Bahujan* and *Zunda.*

2.2 Emergence of Gujarati Dalit Literature

Gujarati Dalit literature started with the Dalit movement initiated in the state. Gujarat Dalit movement received no attention from the mainstream writers. Gujarat Dalit Panther movement was launched by Rameshchandra Parmar in 1975 it marked the advent of the Gujarat Dalit writing. Gujarati Dalit literature had a delayed beginning when compared to Marathi and other states. While in other states the movement of protest towards the upper caste led to the evolution of the Dalit literature but in Gujarat, it didn't evolve out of the larger political movement. In 1981, the anti-caste agitation created a rift between the Gujaratis and Dalits. It was during this period that Gujarat Dalit literature evolved.

Many writings came out into publication with the magazines like *Akrosh, Kalo Sooraj, Garud, Dalit Bandhu, Nayamarg and Disa.* In 1988, Gujarat Dalits established the *Gujarat Dalit Sahitya Academi* it published the quarterly magazines like *Hayati, Samaj Mitra* and *Dalit Chetana.* To encourage the Gujarat Dalit writers the government of Gujarat gives two awards they are Kabir Award for the literary work and Dasi Jeevan award.

Two notable books like *Dalit Literary Tradition in Gujarat: A Critical Study* (2007) written by M.B. Gaijan and *Eklyvaya with Thumbs (*1999) by K.M. Sherrif gives detailed works of different genres in Gujarati literature. The notable writers in poetry are Bipin Gohel's *To the Fading man I sing,* and *To a poet at a Mushaira,* Yoseph Macwan's *A man of No Consequence,* and *A Common Man's Soliloquy,* Kisan Sosa's *The Last Man on Golgotha, Hanging on the Tree, These Men, Dousing the Fire in the Heart,* and *At the Crossroads,* Mangal Rathod's *O, Babasaheb, It is Silent My Friends, Here, Jalsagar,* Narsingh Ujamba's *Words,* Shanker Painter's *To Our Paragons of Virtue, From Broom to Mouth, A Journey by Bus Down the Countryside,* Neerav Patel's *To Our Paragons of Virtue, From Broom to Mouth, A Journey by Bus Down the Countryside,* Pravin Gadhvi's

When Nadir Shah Arrived, Shadow, Mohammed Ishaq Sheikh's *Reflection,* Jayant Parmar's *I am a Man Like You, Identity, Mummy* and Yeshwant Vaghela's *Accident.*

Short story writers also brought out the agony into their writings they are Madhukant Kalpit's *The Unfinished Bridge,* Dalpat Chauhan's *Measure for Measure,* Mohan Parmar's *Slave – labourers,* Harish Mangalam's, *The midwife,* Pathik Parmar's, *Naked Feet,* Naikal Gangera's *Life and Death,* Raghavji Madhad's *Holi* and Dasarath Parmar's *Broken Lid.*

Novel as a form of genre emerged in Gujarat and became a successful form. Joseph Macwan is the first Gujarati writer to win the Kendra Sahitya Academy award for the first novel *Angaliyat* (Step-Child) (1987). After Macwan many writers emerged they are Dalapat Chauhan' '*Malak*' (1991) (The Home –Land), Anjana's (Chaudhary), Harish Mangalam's '*Tirad*' (The Crack) (1992), Mohan Parmar's '*Neliyu*' (The Narrow Lane) (1992), '*Priyatama*' (The Lover) (1995), *Daya Pasha ni Vadi* (A Farm of Daya Pasa) (2003), B. Kesharshivam's '*Shool*' (Thorn) (1995) and *Mool Ane Dhool*'(The source and the Dust), Gunavant Acharya's '*Astitva*' (Existence), Pragaji Bhambhi's '*Diwali Na Divaso*' (Days of Diwali), Daxa Damodara is one women novelist of Gujarat her novels are '*Savitri*', '*Shosh*' (Thirst). The recent work is Vajra Prahar by Kantilal Parmar in 2012.

2.3 Emergence of Tamil Dalit Literature

Tamil Dalit Literature identifying itself as the literature of protest it found its impact on form and content which frequently influenced the language and styles of the writers. The Dalit assertion in South India started in small movements only after the advent of Dalit Panthers in Tamil Nadu in 1982 and Pudiya Tamizhagam in 1998 from then on the many Dalit writers emerged. The book *No Alphabet Insight: New Dalit Writing from South India* edited by Satyanarayana and Susie Tharu in (2011) and the composition of the *Oxford Indian Anthology of Tamil writing* (2012) from 1890-2010 edited by Ravikumar and R.Azhagarasan represents the works of Tamil Dalits. Oxford Anthology consists of 78 selection and 41 writings covering various genres like poetry, fiction, drama, autobiography, biography, prose and archival storage. Iyothee Dasa and Periyar are considered to be the Pioneer in Tamil Dalit literature.

Many magazines like *Dalit Murasu, Puthiya Kondangi, Dalit, Bodhi, Manusanga, Thaiman* and *Adi Tamizhan* were launched into the literary world to bring out the writings of Dalit. Poetry as a major form originated in 1990's. The major poets and their works are Pratibha Jeyachandran, '*The Full Moon will Shine in Village after Village*', '*Dream-teller*' Mathivannan, *'In the Middle of Town', 'What is Possible', Strokes of Gentle Sympathy'* Indiran, *'Wall-posters', 'The City of Burning Slums', 'River'* Mathiazhagan. P, *'The Strategy of Pawns', 'Manhunt'*, N.D. Rajkumar's, *'My Son Wants Me to Buy Him a Toy Car', 'You, My Demon Who Delights in Dancing', 'One Day Long Ago, When the Dying Howl', 'If Anyone Other than Our Own People'* Ravikumar, *'Pond, Where...', 'You, Friend of My Childhood', ' Have You Heard the Rain Crying?'*, Kapilan's, *'Rickshaw Pedalling for Fifteen Years', 'If I Go as Helper in a Construction Job', 'Born to Who knows!'* A. Vincent Raj, *'Clutching the End of Saree'* Thai Kandasamy's *'A Lesson in Action and Reaction', 'Conflict in Friendship', 'A Possibility'*, S. Sukirtharani's *'Portrait of My Village', 'Debt', 'A Faint Smell of Meat', My Body'*, Ku. Umadevi's *'Nirvana's End', 'She Who has Absorbed the Ways', 'Those Who are Protecting this Country'*, Thenmozhi's *'Urn', 'Till Just before Committing that Murder', 'Refusal to Return'*, Yaazhan Athi's, *'Missing', 'Resurrection', He-Goat's Whiskers and Cut-throat Sickle'* Bharathi Nivethan's *'Sensing the Senses'. The Rats have Guts', 'The Lone Woman's'.*

Tamil writers contributed much to other form of the genre the major writers and their works in short stories are Imayam, *'The Binding Vow'*, Azhakiya Periyavan's '*Eardrum*', J.B. Chanakya's *'Force of Gravity'*, Abimani's '*Ailment*', Bama's *'This Man'*, Thenmozhi's *'Paychi Tree'*, Cho. Dharuman's '*Wetness*' Ve. Venkatachalam's *'The Haunted'* Ravikumar's *'Knowing the Truth'*, Sudhakar Kaththak, '*Portrait*'.

The works that belong to Autobiography and Biography are Rettamalai Srinivasan, *'A Brief History of My Life'*, L. Elayaperumal's *'The Flames of Summer'*, Veerammal's *'Ideological Difference with*

Periyar', Bama's '*Karukku*', K.A. Gunasekaran's *'Scar*', Anbu Ponnoviam's *'Pe. Ma. Maduraipillai'*. The works which are in the Archives are Iyothee Thass's *'An Argument Against Conversion', 'A Unique Petition*', Rettamalai Srinivasan's *'Against Conducting ICS Exams in India*', M.C. Rajah, *'Note Submitted to Indian Central Committee*', T.P. Kamalanathan's *'Dalit Leaders' Work in the Field of Education'*. The works on Speeches are Swami Sahajananda's *'Reform Educational Policy*', Meenambal Sivaraj's *'Woman's Advancement is Man's Freedom*', Thol Thirumavalavan's *'Land Rights*', K. Krishnaswamy's *'May the Intoxication of the Film World Clear'*.

The articles that are written in Tamil are Raj Gauthaman's *'Dalit Protest Culture: The First Stage*', Athiyaman's '*Arundhiyars: Problems of Language, Race and Caste Identity'*, P. Sivakami, *'Land: Woman's Breath and Speech'*, Indiran's *'Search for Self in an Urban Jungle: Notes on Contemporary Art'*, G. Chandrasekaran and K.T. Gandhirajan's *'Heritage—Outlines of a Past'*, Stalin Rajangam's *'Dalit Identity: Shades of Approval'*, Thenmozhi's *'Power that Transcends: Physical Body—Societal Body—Dalit Body'*.

The novel became a major form of the genre among the Tamil writers and writers contributed their works only in late 90's. Even the main books like *Oxford Anthology of Tamil writing and No Alphabet Insight* mentioned few works. Imayam's *Koveru Kazhuthaigal* (1994), Poomani's *Piragu* (1979), Bama's *Vanmam Vendetta* (2002) are the major works.

2.4 Emergence of Kannada Dalit Literature

In Karnataka, boosa agitation was the initiative and cradle for the Dalit movement. Dalit Sangharsh Samiti in Karnataka was inaugurated in 1977 from then on the Dalit writing started to emerge. The two major books are D.R. Nagaraja's *The Flamming Feet (2010)* this book focuses on the Dalit movements in Karnataka and the second book *Steel Nibs are Sprouting: A New Dalit Writing from South India, Dossier II* (2013) contributes to the writers works from Kannada and Telugu. As D.R. Nagaraj identifies that the Kannada Dalit writing made its powerful presence in the mid-1970's with the evolution of fiction and poetry.

The famous writers who contributed to various genres are B. Krishnappa, Channanna Walikar, Devanoor Mahadeva, H. Govindaiah, Indurhara Honnapura, Mudnakuda Chinnaswamy, K.B. Siddaiah, Siddalingaiah, Thumbadi Ramaiah, Kotiganahalli Ramaiah, Aravind Malagatti, L. Hanumanthaiah, Mahadeva Shankanapura, Mogalli Ganesh, Subbu Holeyar, B.T. Jahnavi, Du Saraswathi, B.M. Puttaiah, N.K. Hanumanthaiah, Lakkur Ananda, and Bayalu.

The Major works in poetry are Siddalingaiah's *A Song, Thousands of Rivers, My People, The Dalits are Here, Ambedkar, Song of the Cow,* L. Hanumanthaiah's *Mothers, Father,* Du. Saraswathi's *Tip, Tree of Life, The Top,* B.T. Jahnavi's *Adultery, Mother's Cauldron,* Indudhara Honnapura's *What is there in Hindu Dharma?, What does Hindu Dharma Have,* Mudnakuda Chinnaswamy's *To a Rag and Bone Boy,* Subbu Holeyar's *I could have, even now, Killers Drink the Milk of the Cow and With Just One Needle.* Kannada literature gained momentum with novels and Poetry. Devanoora Mahadeva's novels were the famous and some of them are *Tar comes, Inwards, Kusumabale, Untouchability: Great–Grandfather of Apartheid.* M.N. Javaraiah's *Maagi*, Aravind Malagtti's *Kaarya*, Lakshman's *Baduku*, Chennanna Valikara's *Belya* and *Huligemma* and Shivarudra Kallolikar's *Holageriya Rajakumara*.

2.5 Emergence of Telugu Dalit Literature

The Telugu Dalit literature gained its origin with the Karmchedu incident. In the year 1980 two Telugu Dalit journals, *Nalupu* and *Edureeta* were established to contribute the works. Bhagya Reddy organised the first provincial Panchama Mahajana Sabha in Vijayawada in 1917. Kusuma Dharmanna's poetry invoked the Dalit spirit in Andhra. The first anthology of the Telugu Dalit poetry Chikkanavutunna Pata 1995 edited by G. Laxminarsaiah and Tripuraneni Srinivas was launched and later Padunekkina Pata 1966 edited by G. Laxminarsaiah followed the limelight. Both the anthologies did not only confine with the Dalit writing it also had other collections too. Many works followed this anthology they were *Vidi Aakasam* 1999, *Nishani Dikkara Kavita* 1995, *Veliwaada* 1995, *Meerevutlu* 1998, *Chandaludi Chatimpu* in 1996, *Maa oori Maisamma*

1997, *Malle Moggula Godugu* 1999, *Hindu Mahasamudramu* 1996 are the poetry work in the 90's. Women Dalit writers like Gogu shyamala, Joopaka Subhadra, M.M.Vinodini, Jajula Gowri Jally Indira also contributed much to the Telugu Dalit writing in the 80's.

Dalits in Telugu literature is vast and the collection of the writing according to the genre is compiled in polemical books such as *Steel Nibs are Sprouting* 2013 and *The Oxford Indian Anthology of Telugu Dalit writing* 2015. The background study of the Telugu Dalit literature, movements and writers can be seen in *The History of Telugu Dalit literature* 2008 by Thummapudi Bharti.

The Major Telugu writers are Sivasagar, Bojja Tharakam, G. Kalyan Rao, Chilukoori Devaputra, Katti Padma Rao, P. Muthaiah, Sikhamani, M. Satish Chandar, Yendluri Sudhakar, Kalekuri Prasad, Pydi Theresh Babu, Joopaka Subhadra, Madduri Nagesh Babau, Manda Krishna Madiga, Krupakar Madiga, Nagappagari Sunderraju, Challapalli Swaroopa Rani, Gogu Shyamala, Vemula Yellaiah and Jajula Gowri.

Oxford Indian Anthology of Telugu Dalit Literature (2015) gives the list of works on songs they are Jala Rangaswami's *Present Condition of Mala and Madiga*, Nakka Chinavenkaiah's *The Plight of Harijan Women,* Masterjee's *What Kind of Dharma Is this?*, Gaddar's *Oh My Garbage Dump!,* Guda Anjaiah's *The Village Is Ours,* Gorati Venkanna's *The Village Weeps Tears,* Kalekuri Prasad's *The Dowry Pyre,* Nernala Kishore's *Like the Dawn.*

The major works in poetry are Gurram Jashuva's *The Bat Messenger,* Nuthakki Abraham's *Hymn for a Bug,* S.T. Jnanananda Kavi's *Amrapali* Pamu, Ramamurthy's *To the Student,* Modkuri Johnson's *The Crow*, Nadakurthy Swaroopa Rani's *Puzzling Verses for Married Women,* Teresa Devadanam's *I Am a Poet, My Name is Devadanam*, Satish Chandar's *The Fifth Note,* Putla Hemalatha's *The Neighbor,* Taidala Anjaiah's *Our Hut,* Sivasagar's *History in Progress,* Banna Ilaiah's *Undefiled History,* Yendluri Sudhakar's *Autobiography,* G.R. Kurme's *I Was Murdered,* Challapalli Swarupa Rani's *Wild Flower,* Pydi Theresh Babu's *The Great Hindu Ocean,* Chitram Prasad's *To Change The Note*, Madduri Nagesh Babu's *What Caste*

Are You?, J. Goutham's *Wait And See,* G.V. Ratnakar's *Our Children Compete,* Ravinuthala Premkishore's *Yes, We Need to Break This Meal Plate!,* Koyi Koteswar Rao's *Saffron Tree,* Varre Rani's *Python,* Gundedappu Kanakaiah's *O Horror!,* Darla Venkateswara Rao's *In The School Of My Mothers Lap,* Motkupalli Damayanti Devi's *Putrefied Culture,* Sikhamani's *Dark Country,* Inala Saidulu's *The Old Bullock,* Damera Ramulu's *Two Glasses*, *Two Countries,* Kadire Krishna's *The Misaligned, Vastu,* Jupaka Subhadra's *No Guard For My Bosom,* Tullimalli Wilson Sudhakar's *Without You,* Angalakurthi Vidyasagar's *Gleaning The Earth,* Ponnala Balaiah Landa's, *The Crimson Sunrise,* Gogu Shyamala's *Beef, Our Life.*

The list of Short Stories are Boya Jangaiah's *Beware*!, Dara Gopi's *Our Convent*, Kolakaluri Enoch's *Hunger,* Nagappagari Sunder Raju's *Madiga Gundelakka,* Chilukuri Devaputra's *Gurudakshina,* Jajula Gowri's *Bathukamma,* Kannaram Jhansi's *Revenge With Marbles,* Gumpula Venkateshwarlu *Bya Garollu,* Pasunuri Ravinder *Turum Khan.*

The list of Personal Narratives are Bangaru Sridevi's *Why Should I Deny My Caste and My People,* Sujatha Gidla's *From Malapalli To Brahmin Town,* T.N. Sadalakshmi's *The Last Place for a Dalit Woman,* Yelukati Satyanarayana's *His Wife Dies,* Karthik Navayan's *Growing Up In Andhra Pradesh Today,* Gurram Seetharamulu's Bones. Archives works in Telugu are Bhagya Reddy Verma's *How Long Will You Oppress Us?,* Arige Ramaswamy's *Self-Respect of Savarnas,* Kusuma Dharmanna today's, *Crafty Brahmin,* Jeeyar Das's *Controversy Over the Meeting At Visakhapatnam*, P.R. Venkatswamy's *Dedication of Devadasis,* B. Shyamsunder's *Where Do Muslims Stand Today?,* J. Eshwaribai's *In Andhra Pradesh, Legislative Assembly.*

The works on essays are Bojja Tarakam's *Ayodhya and the Hindus,* Katti Padma Rao's *The Historical Context of the Karamchedu Movement,* Ghanta Chakrapani's *The Dalit Has Conquered the World,* K.S. Chalam's *Tantra,* P. Muthaiah's *Dandora: The Triple-Identity Movement,* Jilukara Srinivas's *Village: The Social Prison,* B. Vijayabharathi's *Tataka,* K. Satyanarayana's *Dalitism: a Critique of Telugu Literature*, M.M. Vinodini's *Teaching Tormenting Texts,*

Gundimeda Sambaiah's *Claiming Right to Represent and Agency: Dalits and Public Sphere,* M.F. Gopinath's *Dalits and Left Intellectuals,* P. Kesava Kumar's *Song: The Voice of the Voiceless.*

Kaki Bakthalu by Parsavokarasan could be the first Dalit novel from Telugu. Dalit Novel of 1980's is *Panchamam* by Chillukuri Deviputhra, *Muinchi nila bhavi* by Sadhanandha Saradha, Vemulu Yellais *Kakka*, Kalyana Rao's *Antarani vasantham* (Untouchable Spring), *Sahu and Allam Rajaiya's Komaram beem* is another novel from Telugu Novels were written even before the decades of Independence Jala Rangaswami published *Raitupilla* and *Dunnevanniki Bhoomi* in 1920's itself. G. Kalyan Rao's *Untouchable spring* brings forth the seven generations of the Dalit life to the readers and Vemula Yellaiah's *Kaka* deals with the Telangana dialect, orality and Dalit diction is portrayed in the novels and both the novels were published in 2000 which are noteworthy novels in the Telugu Dalit Literature.

2.6 Emergence of Malayalam Dalit Literature

The Kerala Dalit literature emerged only in the late 1970's and the reason for the late appearance is due to the Renaissance in Kerala. *Ramacharitam* is considered to be the first written poem in Malayalam in the fourteenth century. In the later part of the sixteenth century, Thunchath Ezhuthachan was considered to be the father of Malayalam language as his works were so memorable and his forms of poetry supported for the welfare of the low caste. Nambiar localised the art form and he created the art form called as *Thullal* and used the local language and dialect of the Dalits.

The major writers in Malayalam poetry are Poikayil Appachan's, *Songs by Poikayil Appachan,* K.K. Govindan's, *The Killing Field,* Kaviyoor Murali's, *The Gospel for Dalits,* K.K.S. Das's, *My Soil, The Black Lane*, Raghavan Atholi's, *Justice Cooked, Where Hunger is Sold,* Sunny, Kavikkad's, *An Uncharted Map*, G. Sasi Madhuraveli's, *With Love, Mother,* S. Jospeh's, *Group Photo, Some Dark Success*, Sivadas Purameri's, *Some Types of Fingers, A Leaky Room*, M.R. Renukumar's, *The Silent Beast, The Poison Fruit,* M.B. Manoj's, Survey of India, Mothers, O, Ant, O Paddystalk, Vijila's *A Place for*

Me, I Can't Grow my Nails, The Autobiography of a Bitch and Binu. M Pallipad's Six Philosophers Untie to Exclude Amavasi from the Play.

The famous short fiction writers are T.K.C. Vaduthala's, *Sweet Offering at Chankaranthy,* Paul Chirakkarode's, *Nostalgia*, C. Ayyappan's, *Madness*, P.A. Uthaman's, *The Story of a Sickle*, P.K. Prakash's, *Luminious White*, M.K. Madhukumar's *Paalakkunnan's Journey.*

Some of the autobiography and biography writers are Kallen Pokkudan's, *My Life,* Velayudhan Panikkasseri's, *Excerpts from Ayyankali*, K.T. Rajkumar's, *Poikayil Sreekumara Guru- A Historical record*, T.H.P. Chentharasseri's, *Pampadi John Joseph*, Elikulam Jayakumar's *Kallara Sukumaran* and Taha Madayi's *Adiyar Teacher*.

The short stories arrived in 1824 they are *Oru Kuttiyudan Maranam*, *Aaneyeyum Thunnaneyum Kurichulla Katha*, *Oru kallan*, *Vasana Vikriti*. *Red volunteer, Nikshepam, Ghoshayatra, Vallikaadevi* Pulayas Jaatheeyatha, Chankranthi Ada, Randu Thalamura. The major plays were Varma Valiya Koyi Thampuran's *Abijnana Shakunthalam*, *Adukkalayilninnu Arangathekku,* Pattabakki, *Balakalesam*, *Naadugaddika*.

Novels had its beginning in 80's it started with the translation of Richard Collin's *The Slayer Slain into Ghathakavadham* in 1878. *Pullerikunju* in 1882 by Archdeacon Koshy, *Sukumari* by Mooliyil Joseph in 1897, Chori Peter's *Parishkaara Vijayam* in 1906 are the notable novels. Many other works like Thakazhi Sivasankara Pillai who is called as Kerala's Mulk Raj Anand work's *Randidangazhi* in 1945 and *Thottiyude Makan* in 1947, Nagavally R.S. Karup's *Thotti* 1947, Kesava Dev's *Kannadi* 1973 are the works which speak the economic condition of the Dalits. Paul Chirakkarode, Vaduthala's contemporary, almost nine deal with Dalit issues. *Pulayathara, Mathil, Nizhal, Nyayasana, Velicham* (three volumes), and many other novels were written by Chirakkarode. D. Rajan's novel *Mukkani* is a literary representation of Paraya life. T.C.K. Vaduthala with his works like Kattayum Koythum, Nanavulla Mannu and Changalakal Nurungunnu brought out the Dalit political power in the fiction. Other major works in novels are T.K.C. Vaduthala's *When Shackles Break,* D. Rajan's *The Festival at Muthan Kavu,* Paul Chirakkarode's *The Pulaya Ghetto,* P.A. Uthaman's *The Death Wali and* Raghavan Atholi's *Legacy of Blood.*

2.7 Emergence of Dalit Literature in Punjab

The emergence of the Dalit literature in Punjab started with the Ad-Dharm movement by Mangoon Ram. Poets emerged in the twentieth century they were Charan Das Nidharhak, Gurdas Ram Alam, Chanan Lal Manik, Sant Ram Udasi, Manmohan and Pritam Ramdaspuri. Gurcharan Singh's *Mashalchi* is the first Dalit novel in Punjab and the other novels are Sohan Singh Sital's *Jug Badal Gaya*, Jaswant Singh Kanwal *Hani* and Gurdial, Singh's *Marhi Da Deeva.* Punjab autobiographies are written by young writers like Laxaman Gaikwad's *Uchakka* and Balbir's *Chhangya.* Short stories such as the works of Bhagwant Rasoolpuri's *Jarhan* and *Ad-Danka* were written in 2010.

2.8 Emergence of Dalit Literature in Odisha

Odisha is not a stranger to the suppression and untouchability like the other states. Oriya Dalit literature also started with the advent of Buddhism. The major works started to emerge during the fifteenth century and the Bhima Bhoi movement made the rage stronger in the nineteenth century. Harijan Sevak Sangha was started in the year 1978 to support the Dalits. Sudramuni Sarala Dasa was the pioneer of the social protest movement in the fifteenth Century and her major works are *Oriya Mahabharata, Bilanka Ramayana* and *Chandi Purana.*

The other poets who protested against the atrocities during 1450-1550 are the five fellow poets named as Balarama Dasa, Jagannatha Dasa, Achyutananda Dasa, Jasobanta Dasa and Ananta Dasa. Their works were *Jagmohan Ramayan, Laxmi Puran, Oriya Bhagabata, Harivamsa, Premabhakti Brahmagita and Hetudaya Bhagabata.* Once again the protest literature was retrieved by Bhima Bhoi and his notable works were *Stuti Chintamani, Srutinisedha Gita and Nibeda Sadhana.* Late in the twentieth century the Oriya people started to focus on different forms of genres until then they focused on poetry and the poets who protested against the casteism are Basudev Sunani,

Kumaramani Tanti, Sanjay Bag, Anjubala Jena and Mohan Jena. The notable short story in Oriya is Ramachandra Sethi's *Dwitiya Buddha* (The Second Buddha).

2.9 Features of the Dalit Novel

Dalit literature itself is the literature of protest and it gives voice to the voiceless. The originality of the Dalit novel lies in its setting. The characters are common people and not of aristocratic class and they converse about the common issues, not about Nation and its Politics. Coming to the setting, one can see the characters involve in conversation at cowshed, at church, at Village Panchayat, in the fields or where their fellow Caste people come across each other. The Dalit novel doesn't follow the three unities of time which are a conventional method applied to study the Indian English novel. The Dalit novel presents the events unevenly and as per the demand of the situation. We find the repetition of the incidents in the Dalit novel.

The Dalit novel makes the reader understand that insecure childhood, ever dependence for the assistance of the government, socio-cultural oppression, gender dominance, exploitation in paying the daily wages, sexual harassment at the workplaces and physical attacks, police cases and political influence are the day-to-day experiences of the Dalits. We can also see the Dalit characters are passive once they move away from their living areas to that of the Caste Hindus. The experience of alienation and otherness are commonly found incidents in the Dalit novel. The Dalit novel succinctly depicts the aspects of the social exclusion and the cultural dominance that the Dalit experience due to the oppressive Hindu social order.

The protagonist of the Dalit novel is a commoner and not of heir or heiress to take the lead of the Dalit communities. The champion of the Dalit community is identified in the course of time as each character is introduced to the appreciation of the reader. The protagonist of a Dalit novel may not be a well educated, rich in prosperity as well as in employment instead he or she is the one who takes a righteous stand for developing his or her own Caste people. The protagonist of the Dalit novel is the one who readily faces the challenges and empowers his or her people. The protagonist stands as a role model for his Caste.

Apart from dealing with the above-mentioned issues, the Dalit novel is of rich experiences of the Dalits and paved the way for the formation of their collective consciousness rightly identifying themselves to fight against the Caste and Gender hierarchy.

2.10 Emergence of Gujarati Dalit Novel

The novel as a form of genre emerged in Gujarat and became a successful form Joseph Macwan is the first Gujarati writer to win the Kendra Sahitya Akademy award for the first novel *Angaliyat* (Step-Child) (1987). After Macwan many writers emerged they are Dalapat Chauhan' '*Malak*' (1991) (The Home –Land), Anjana's (Chaudhary), Harish Mangalam's '*Tirad*' (The Crack) (1992), Mohan Parmar's '*Neliyu*' (The Narrow Lane) (1992), '*Priyatama*' (The Lover) (1995), *Daya Pasha ni Vadi* (A Farm of Daya Pasa) (2003), B. Kesharshivam's '*Shool*' (Thorn) (1995) and *'Mool Ane Dhool'*(The source and the Dust), Gunavant Acharya's '*Astitva*' (Existence), Pragaji Bhambhi's '*Diwali Na Divaso*' (Days of Diwali), Daxa Damodara is one women novelist of Gujarat her novels are '*Savitri*', '*Shosh*' (Thirst). The recent work is *Vajra Prahar* by Kantilal Parmar in 2012.

2.11 Emergence of Tamil Dalit Novel

The novel became a major form of the genre among the Tamil writers and writers contributed their works only in late 90's. Even the main books like *Oxford Anthology of Tamil writing and No Alphabet Insight* mentioned few works. Imayam's *Koveru Kazhuthaigal* (1994) Poomani's *Piragu* (1979), Bama's *Vanmam Vendetta* (2002) are the major works.

2.12 Emergence of Kannada Dalit Novel

Devanoora Mahadeva's novels were the famous and some of them are *Tar comes, Inwards, Kusumabale, Untouchability: Great–Grandfather of Apartheid*. M.N. Javaraiah's *Maagi*, Aravind Malagtti's *Kaarya*, Lakshman's *Baduku*, Chennanna Valikara's *Belya* and *Huligemma* and Shivarudra Kallolikar's *Holageriya Rajakumara*.

2.13 Emergence of Telugu Dalit Novel

Kaki Bakthalu by Parsavokarasan could be the first Dalit novel from Telugu. Dalit Novel of 1980's is *Panchamam* by Chillukuri Deviputhra, *Muinchi nila bhavi* by Sadhanandha Saradha, Vemulu Yellais *Kakka*, Kalyana Rao's *Antarani vasantham* (Untouchable Spring), *Sahu and Allam Rajaiya's Komaram beem* is another novel from Telugu Novels were written even before the decades of Independence Jala Rangaswami published *Raitupilla* and *Dunnevanniki Bhoomi* in 1920's itself. G. Kalyan Rao's *Untouchable spring* brings forth the seven generations of the Dalit life to the readers and Vemula Yellaiah's *Kaka* deals with the Telangana dialect, orality and Dalit diction is portrayed in the novels and both the novels were published in 2000 which are noteworthy novels in the Telugu Dalit Literature.

2.14 Emergence of Malayalam Dalit Novel

Novels had its beginning in 80's it started with the translation of Richard Collins *The Slayer Slain* into *Ghathakavadham* in 1878. *Pullerikunju* in 1882 by Archdeacon Koshy, *Sukumari* by Mooliyil Joseph in 1897, Chori Peter's *Parishkaara Vijayam* in 1906 are the notable novels. Many other works like Thakazhi Sivasankara Pillai who is called as Kerala's Mulk Raj Anand work's *Randidangazhi* in 1945 and *Thottiyude Makan* in 1947, Nagavally R.S. Karup's *Thotti* 1947, Kesava Dev's *Kannadi* 1973 are the works which speak the economic condition of the Dalits. Paul Chirakkarode, Vaduthala's contemporary, almost nine deal with Dalit issues. *Pulayathara, Mathil, Nizhal, Nyayasana, Velicham* (three volumes), and many other novels were written by Chirakkarode. D. Rajan's novel *Mukkani* is a literary representation of Paraya life. T.C.K. Vaduthala with his works like Kattayum Koythum, Nanavulla Mannu and Changalakal Nurungunnu brought out the Dalit political power in the fiction. Other major works in novels are T.K.C. Vaduthala's *When Shackles Break,* D. Rajan's *The Festival at Muthan Kavu,* Paul Chirakkarode's *The Pulaya Ghetto,* P.A. Uthaman's *The Death Wali* and Raghvan Atholi's *Legacy of Blood.*

2.15 Emergence of Dalit Novel in Punjabi

Gurcharan Singh's *Mashalchi* is the first Dalit novel in Punjab.

Sohan Singh Sital's work *Jug Badal Gaya* is a novel and other major novelist in Punjab are Jaswant Singh Kanwal and his work *Hani* and Gurdial Singh's *Marhi Da Deeva.* Dwarka Barthi is well known Dalit writer of Punjab.

2.16 Emergence of Marathi Dalit Novel

All forms of genres other than novel are worked but novel gained its importance only in late twentieth century some novels are Sharnkumar Limable's *Hindu* (2010), *Upalya, Bahujan,* and *Zunda.*

2.17 Select Dalit Novels: Synoptical View

The scholar has selected six Dalit novels for her study. The novels are placed from different states of India and it deals with the different problems and sufferings of the Dalits. The select novels for the research are Joseph Macwan's *Step Child* (2004) from Gujarat, Bama's *Vanmam Vendetta* (2008) from Tamil Nadu, Sharan kumar Limbale's *Hindu* (2010) from Maharashtra, G. Kalyan Rao's *The Untouchable spring* (2010) from Andhra Pradesh, P. Sivakami's *The Taming of Women* (2012) form Tamil Nadu, and Kancha Ilaiah's *Untouchable God* (2013) from Telungana.

2.17.1 Joseph Macwan's *The Stepchild* (2004)

Joseph Macwan's novel *The Stepchild* (1987) was the first Gujarat Dalit novel originally written in Gujarati in the year 1987 and it won the National Sahitya Academy award in the year 1988. After a decade and a half, the novel got translated by Rita Kothari and published in English in the year 2004. Joseph Macwan writes in his acknowledgment that there is no dearth of literature about the higher castes in Gujarat but most of the life experiences of the common people find no reflection at all. Sufferings want, pain, exploitation, social injustice- the marginalisation Dalit community is continuously victimised by all these evils and yet it has a culture of its own, a unique tradition of living its own adventures and tales of courage. Mainstream literature has not even touched these aspects. Filling this gap in Gujarat- though it may sound like self-praise- is what I have done. Angaliyat is a symbol of this attempt.

Joseph Macwan was born in Tranol near Kunjarav in Anand district on October 9, 1935. He is a well known Gujarati writer who received National Sahitya Academy Award 1988 for his novel Angaliyat. He has 40 books including 14 novels and 9 character sketches to his credits. He was the President of Gujarati Dalit Sahitya Academy. He passed away on 28th March 2010.

2.17.2 Bama's Vanmam-vendetta (2008)

Bama's Vanmam was originally written in Tamil in the year 2002 it got later translated into English by R. Azhagarasan and published in the year 2008. Faustina Mary Fatima Rani was born in the year 1958 in Phudapatti in Madras. She became famous through her autobiography Karuku in 1992 and then she started publishing novels like *Sangati* (1994) and *Vanmam* (2002) and her other works are *Kusumbukkaran* (1996) (Short Stories) *Oru Tattvum Erumaiyum* (2003).

Bama states in her novel Vanmam-Vendetta (2002) about the rift and quarrel between Pallars and Parayas. A small rift caused by the uppercastes make women suffer and later how the women manage to lead their life without the help of men and how they speak out bravely to the police about the murder and injustice happened to them shows the strength of the women in the novel. United they are and make history by capturing power for the very first time from the entrenched dominant caste leadership. The major characters in this novel are Swaminathan, Palaniswamy Naiker, Ranga Naiker, Karupuswamy, Sethuraman, Jayaraju. The time is cyclic in narration, and the themes involved in this novel are sub-caste discrimination and gender discrimination.

2.17.3 Sharankumar Limbale's Hindu (2010)

Sharankumar Limable is a well known Marathi Dalit writer born on June 1st, 1956. He is well known for his autobiography *Outcaste*. He has 40 books to his credits and his book *Towards the Aesthetics of Dalit literature* traces about the background, evolution and cultural aspects of the Dalits. He has written the first Dalit Marathi novel *Hindu* and it was translated into English by Arun Prabha Mukherjee in 2010.

This novel Hindu seeks to highlight the power politics and further consequences that lead to the killing of a Dalit youth, raping of a Dalit woman and further legal operations from both the caste Hindus and the Dalits. The struggle for power is being depicted in this novel Hindu and how a Dalit suffers from becoming a leader and what are the conspiracies made behind it and how the upper-class people dominate and oppress the lower caste people to get hold of power is narrated in this novel. Finally, the author proves to the society that leaders are not born by birth they are made to become leaders by the people. As Lincoln stated that the rule of democracy is 'For the people, of the people and by the people. The characters in this novel are Madhukur Kavale, Prabakar Kavale, Tatya Kamble, Sadhanand Kamble, Miland. The setting is in Alachpur and the narrative style is linear. The themes dealt are Caste discrimination, power politics, rivalry, gender discrimination.

2.17.4 G. Kalyan Rao's Untouchable Spring (2010)

Kalyan Rao is a distinguished writer in Telugu. He is the author of Aruna Tara magazine which portrays current and prevalent issues, related to Dalits in Andhra Pradesh. He holds an esteemed position in the Vi Ra Sam (Revolutionary Writers Association). His novel Antarani Vasantham was written in Telugu and was translated into English as Untouchable Spring in the year 2010 by Alladi Uma and M. Sridhar.

The novel deals with a family of Dalits for seven generations. It brings the rich and vibrant cultural traditions of Dalit community. It clearly states about the Dalit identity. There are 18 chapters in the novel and the first 14 chapters are seriously dedicated to exploring the agony of Dalits but when it turns to 15th chapter the story suddenly takes a climax of introducing Naxalism in the novel. It portrays about the generation of struggles faced by the Dalit community in the clutches of the upper caste people. Finally, the change in religion and education uplifts the lifestyle of the Dalits. It's a historical document, illustrates the plight of Dalits in a post-independence era. The writer is of revolutionary ideology and he portrays the Dalit Christians and their humiliation in the hands of caste Hindus. The novel runs with the recollection of repeated memories. The setting is in Andhra Pradesh in a small village of Yennela Dinni, Pakkela Dinni. The major characters are Yellenna, Naganna, Narigadu and the theme dealt is the caste discrimination.

2.17.5 P. Sivakami's The Taming of Women (2012)

P. Sivagami born in 1957 is an acclaimed Tamil writer. She is the first Tamil Dalit women to become a novelist. She has written four critically acclaimed novels all of them centred on Dalit and feminist themes. In literary circles, P. Sivakami is considered as a strong Dalit writer with a feminist penchant. She is founder editor of literary magazine Puthiya Kodangi. In 2009, she founded her own political party, samuga samathuva padai. Originally written in Tamil, it has been translated into English by Pritham K. Chakravarthy in the year 2012.

The novel traces about the suffering of women and especially Dalit women under the pangs of the Dalit men. She openly throws the reality of women who faces the discrimination under the hands of both upper caste men and from the men of their own caste. However, radical the woman she is always made to be under the control of men is clearly depicted in this novel. The major characters are Anandhayi, Periyannan and the themes dealt are caste discrimination, denial of education and male domination. The setting is not mentioned in the novel as the author tries to put forth her view that the women face the discrimination of the men in all the walk of life everywhere.

2.17.6 Kancha Ilaiah's Untouchable God (2013)

Kancha Ilaiah was born on 5 October 1952. He is an Indian academician, writer and activist for Dalit rights. He has published eight books and a good number of articles in reputed journals. He has been a recipient of the Mahatma Jyotirao Phule Award and was a Nehru Fellow between, 1994-97. Currently, he is working in Maulana Azad National Urdu University, Hyderabad.

His novel *Untouchable God* was originally written in English by him in the year 2013. In the novel, he talks about the six upper caste men from different state join together for a feast and they celebrate the death of the Dalit. The themes dealt in this novel are caste discrimination, gender discrimination, and religious oppression.

In chapter–2, I have tried to bring out the synoptical view of the select Dalit novels besides dealing with the definition and the key aspects of Dalit novel. I have also tried to provide a detailed list of the available Dalit novels in English which are translated from their respective regional languages. Chapter–3 entitled "Writing the Caste Discrimination and Alienation" deals with how the Dalits in India have been discriminated in the name of caste and further how the elements of caste-based discriminatory approaches have become adoptive for showing their dominance over the Dalits by the caste Hindus. I have also analysed how the caste-based discrimination and alienation have been succinctly depicted through certain imaginary characters and situations in the select novels.

Chapter - 3

Writing the Caste Discrimination and Alienation

Chapter 3 deals with the form and nature of caste discrimination executed by the caste-Hindus and how the caste and religious modes of hegemony made the Dalits to feel self-alienation from the mainstream society. The chapter also deals with how the Dalits are humiliated and exploited at every walk of their life and how the select novels made an uncompromised attempt to represent the plights of the Dalits using certain images and symbols which are not yet addressed by the mainstream Indian English novelists.

3.1 Joseph Macwan's The Stepchild

Angaliyat (1987) is a Gujarati Dalit novel written by Joseph Macwan. The novel portrays the sufferings, resistance, anguish, desire, pain, exploitation, social injustice of the marginalised communities. As Joseph Macwan himself states that "*Angaliyat* (1987) is a tale of a culture that is extinct and pushed into oblivion on purpose. It is not an attempt to re-establish its prestige but to acknowledge and sing of its strength and character". *Angaliyat* is the first Gujarati novel written in 1987 and in 1988 it received the National Sahitya Akademi award. The novel is translated into English as *The Stepchild* (2004) by Rita Kothari. *Angaliyat* is the novel of the revolt of lower caste people (Vankarvas) against the upper caste people (Patels). In this novel the character, Teeho is the young and rebellious man who fights for the humiliations of Vankarvas as he is not able to tolerate the atrocities which are imposed on his caste people. He has the courage in the heart to face the Patels and his revolutionary attitude never subdues till his death.

The novel is about the community of weavers, the Vankars, is subject to oppression from the more powerful upper caste of the Patels in Gujarat. The author has drawn the incidents which happened in the real life of the community of the weavers in Gujarat. The setting of the novel is in the author's own place Anand district. The thematic concern of the novel are: the lifestyle of the people in local idioms, the gripping tale of love, heroism, humiliation, revenge and death. The opening of the novel is so strong by portraying the discrimination of caste between the Patels and Vankarvas.

Vaseemahmed G Qureshi (2013) states that Angaliyat works on four levels. It is a gripping tale of love, heroism, humiliation, revenge and death. It is a vividly coloured picture of the lives of two neighbouring villages in the Charotar district of central Gujarat. It is a document of the politics of the pre- and post-Independence years, as seen from the perspective of the downtrodden; and finally, it is an account of the struggle of one dalit community against its upper-caste oppressors, spurred on by two opposing ideologies, the Gandhian and the Ambedkarite. The first incident which ignited the caste discrimination continue till the end of the novel with bloodshed, revenge and murder taking the life of the poor Vankarva men Teeho and his community men. The setting of the novel takes place in three villages like Shilapur, Ratnapur and Kedaria. As the enmity between the Patels and Vankarvas leads to the enmity of the people in neighbouring villages and they are pushed into an alienated surrounding leading to the exclusion of the people from entering the villages.

Teeho the main protagonist of the novel with his friend Valji goes for auction in Shilapaar they come across the incident where an upper caste man Patel cast a stone on the pot of charming young Vankarva woman Methi. She was drenched and abashed and around her feet the broken pot was shattered. Methi uttered "Bastard, which mother produced an evil son? Mind your bloody language… you slut!" (SC 15) said the Patels and by saying so the men's eyes started to rove over the women's nipples visible through her wet blouse. This humiliated Teeho and he went forward to question the men who were Patels but he and his companions asked him to be calm and asked him "you mind your own business, outsider!" The fellow raised his voice to snub Teeho". (SC 16) But Teeho attacked the upper caste man and his companions. The trouble maker's companion got angry and came forward to attack Teeho "A low-caste man publicly humiliating an upper-caste, a Patel no less! How could anyone allow this?" (SC 16)Teeho grabbed him by the collar and threw him around. The village Mukhi arrived at the spot and he was aware of the situation and its happenings. Megho Patel told the Mukhi that "You are the Mukhi. I want to file a police complaint against this *dhed (*low-caste). The situation went out of control and the upper caste men started attacking Teeho and he was wounded with blood stain. Through this incident, the discrimination is seen very evident and the Dalit women are always under the lascivious gaze of the upper caste men though their caste is untouchable but their body is not so.

The Caste discrimination leads to the alienation as Teeho felt so bad that no one from his community came forward from Shilapur to say "Teehabhai, you have saved us from disrepute" he understood that no one wanted to be on the wrong side of the Patidars:

> Teeho was aware of this' in fact it filled him with contempt. The entire Mohalla consisted of eighty houses. If all of them stood united, the twenty-five families of the Patels would be powerless, but if they couldn't even dream of standing up for themselves, how were they to face the Patels? The money was with the Patels, in fact, as far as money was concerned, even the Thakore depended upon the Patels. In such circumstances to pick a fight with them was impractical and foolish. (SC 18)

Methi meets Teeho and invites him home. Moti, her bother said that "But you know how it is- first of all our caste is a low one, and then one can't live in water and risk enmity with the crocodile". (SC 19) The brutality of the Patels had no boundaries and they wanted to take revenge on Teeho "The Patels argued that if a low-caste man and an outsider at that had publicly beaten up a Patel's son, he must be taught a lesson for life" (SC 26) In India, it is under the pretext of the Caste and in the Western World, it is under the name of the Race.

Inequality is the main source of marginality which leads to insecurity, injustice and exploitation.

The Patels went to the extent of destroying the life of the Vankarvas people. The enmity which started in Shilapaar when Teeho attacked the Patels it arose to many problems in and around the villages. In this novel Macwan puts forth that the enmity of one Dalit men with the upper caste men leads to the destruction of the whole community. On account of one man's protest against the upper caste, the whole community undergoes the suffering. If a Dalit rebels against the upper caste men it is not an individual struggle within him the whole community is voicing out. Macwan brings out the series of atrocities which are carried out by the upper caste people over the Dalit to destroy the peace of the community as a whole. The Patels destroyed the land of Heera Khana in Shilapur and they hung a threatening note that:

> If you have anything to do with any of your community members in Ratnappar or let any of them enter here, that will be your end. You will be thrown out of the village, without even a drop of water from the lake. If you wish to live in this village harmoniously, then let Moti Dhula and Heera Khana be ostracized and made to answer for their conduct! (SC 29)

The love and marriage portrayed in this novel are so intense and the relationships are very loyal to each other. The love between Teeho and Methi is so intense and they fall in love with each other at first sight though they belong to different paragna. They even go to the extent of marrying each other. The Patel's plan to ruin the love which Methi and Teeho had developed and were waiting for a good time to spoil it "She goes around like a sati, let her be saddled with this one, it will straighten her up for life. If Teeha has to live this knowledge, his life will be miserable. There is no punishment worse than this". (SC 38) The evil intention of raping Methi underwent a change instead they planned to ruin her future. They called Methi's child marriage husband Chunthia and ignited him "we have heard that Heera is not arranging the aanu and somebody from another paragna are making plans to elope with your wife. The caste may be yours, but our village will earn a bad reputation! This kind of thing had never happened before in any Caste. We have not let it happen. And even now we don't want it to happen". (SC 39) For which Chunthia never agreed and said "You think I am a worm, don't you? Who asked you to take the responsibility of my aanu? I spit on your money…!' His words infuriated Meghi, his nephew Manji and his worthless son Nanio and Nanji said "Look at that! What arrogance for a bloody dhedh!" (SC 40) Through this incident, one can get to know how the life of a Dalit is put to difficult times personally, socially and psychologically when they try to voice out against the upper caste people. The Patels indirectly ignite the fire within the community of the Dalits to spoil the harmony and peacefulness.

The upper caste men join together to spoil the life of the lower caste men and their indirect vengeance in reducing the harmony of the Vankarvas is depicted through an incident where Valji Teeho's friend plans to make a secret way to fix Methi's wedding. He asked Dano to help for fixing the taxi to bring Methi in the night but when they approached Gola he never accepted for helping them even when they accepted to pay thrice the amount. Then Dano remembered the help which Dhelavala promised that he would do when he caught him in the night with Ramlo having sex. He never spread about it to the villagers so Dhelavala said "Look, Dana, you seem to be a useful person. Ask for my help when you are struck someday. I will not turn you down". (SC 72) So he approached him but he too played a cunning role as he is giving a helping hand but he spread the message to Meghiji and the plan got collapsed. Instead of Dano and Valji it was Manji and Nanji takes Methi to Keradia and when Valji tries to rescue her he was beaten to death. Dalit always live a pitiful life their life is always tested by the upper caste men. Though the discrimination is not seen directly but making use of the situation the upper caste men indirectly plan to ruin the life of a Dalit. Dalits are treated as mere animals as their life has no value under the casteist fangs of the upper caste men.

The discrimination which started with the Dalit voicing out leads to many incidents, as Teeho was not allowed to enter the Shilapur village for auction anymore. The fight between the Patels and Vankarvas lead to the separation of the neighbouring village. The discrimination leads to alienation and exclusion of the Dalits not to enter Shilapur. Even within Ratnapur Teeho was being alienated.

Making use of the exclusion from the village the Patels secretly writes a letter to Heera like Teeho asking Methi to get married and not to wait anymore. After seeing the letter Methi gets married to Chunthia and Teeho remained unmarried. Even after so many years, it is Teeho who saves her and child when she tries to commit suicide as she is vexed of marriage life with Chunthia. Even at that point of time they never felt like starting a life together. As far as concerned the love between Teeho and Methi it was not just a physical but it was more of pure eternal love.

The Stepchild (2004) is the novel written during the independence period and the author Joseph Macwan brings out the pre-independence and post-independence struggles of the Dalits. It was during this period the Dalits as one community fought against the British and on the other hand they fought against the internal oppression imposed by the caste Hindus within the country. The upper caste men always try to bring money, women, politics under the control of them through their casteist ideologies. Though Gujarat, being a Gandhian born nation the ideologies of Ambedkar gained momentum in the hearts of the Dalits. Gandhi supported Dalits as it was merely for the political favour. Gandhi's idea was not to make Dalits rebellious as it would break the country. And the population of the Hindus was less compared to the Dalits. So whenever the Dalits were in need of help Gandhi granted it but Ambedkar didn't want the favour of Gandhi as Ambedkar felt that the Dalits need self-respect, equality, justice, dignity and self-identity to voice out for the rights of their birth.

Gandhian support for Dalits for the sake of independence of the nation is seen evident by making the law in favour of them. The Patels felt that they can do anything with money and power but in this novel whoever does the crime are being punished while the law never works in favour of the caste, power, or people. When the upper-caste people destroyed Heera's fields with the help of Master, an educated man Valji and Teeho met the Collector and explained the whole incidents which took place in Shilapaar. The next day police came to arrest the people who destroyed the field and asked Teeho to give the names of the people without fear of who attacked him and destroyed the fields of Heera. For which Teeho replied:

> To tell the truth Saheb, I am not at all afraid of anybody. Why should I be afraid when we have a government of people like you? If they confront me one at a time I would relish even dying in the process. It's just that difficult to cope with the harassment of our people and conspiracies that take place behind our backs. (SC 48)

Through Teeho's words, the internal fight among the community of the Dalits is visible. Within the community itself, the people don't have a unity which makes the upper caste people take the strand to create a rift between the Dalits. When Valji was killed, the police went to Keradia and rescued Methi and arrested the people who were behind the death of Valji:

> Manji, Nanji and Gola were found guilty on the charges of conspiracy and execution of the murder of Valji, and were sentenced to life. Dehlavala was made to serve internment for a month and a half and charged with a fine of 1000 rupees for playing an indirect role in the conspiracy. On the other hand, Meghji Patel and Khushlo were given the benefit of doubt since there was no evidence of their direct and indirect involvement. (SC 105)

When the riot between Jeevan and Dehlavala's car driver Ramlo broke out there was a huge rage in Ratnapaar. The people started attacking each other and they were searching for Jeevan with blood rage. Dano Jeevan and Teeho went to the master and told about the whole situation. Master picked them to the police station the DSP never responded properly to the situation since they were under Dehlavala's control. Master asked the driver to go to Ahmedabad. Master went and met Gandhiji's senior followers and told about the happenings in Ratnapaar and about Dehlavala. Within that day all arrangements were made and a letter from Regional President reached Dehlavala stating that he should ask forgiveness to the Vankarvas and later it will be reported whether he will be allowed to continue or dismiss the party. Before Master left he said to Dehlavala that "The sun of Gandhi Bapu is still warm in this country, Dehlavala". (SC 201)

The upper caste men in order to gain the prestigious and dignified position put up a mask to be in favour of the Dalits and involve themselves in the moment to fight against atrocities. Dehlavala in the process of fighting the case and plowing money of his own is the country struggle for freedom he made contacts with senior national leaders. When English government imprisoned the leader Dehlavala put up conspicuous 'British Quit India' posters in appreciation of his service Congress appointed him as a representative on District Local Board. Dehlavala was the only person who had a car. He appoints Harijan Ramla as his car driver to show that he has no discrimination among people.

Even after so many years when Teeha enters into the town for auction, he was beaten up to death. "Eight to ten young men came crashing down upon Teeha. With sticks and punches, they left Teeha half dead". (SC 226). The violence of the caste can be seen evidently in this novel. As the spark which was ignited years ago still continues and the rage of casteism comes to an end with the murder. But still it is not abolished fully until the final root of the family is destroyed.

As the novel to its name *The Stepchild* (2004) deals with two different incidents which bring out the significance of the title through the character Valji and Goku who face internal discrimination being considered outsiders within the community. Valji's mother Monghi was the second wife of Bijal. After few days of marriage, Monghi had gone back to her parents and been divorced. Bijal had fallen in love with Monghi and a month after the divorce they were married. Valji was born in the seventh month. People took it in a wrong and said that "Valo is not Bijal's child, he is from the previous house. He was born here, that's all. Otherwise he is definitely an angaliyat" (SC 68) These words made Bijal angry and he sent word to the Brahmin and to all mohalla to have meal in their household and he stated that "Those who consider Valji as his son may come, the rest who think he is an angaliayat can stay away!" (SC 68) Everyone came home and had the meal though they had a diverse opinion towards the child they kept calm and never talked about it. Valji still feels that "I can't get this damn thorns out of my flesh- how long will the world consider me an outsider?" (SC 69)

In an another incident after rescuing Methi and her child, Teeho gives shelter to them, but Patels and their children make fun of Goku as Stepchild to Teeho. Goku complains to Teeho that Ramlo's and Bikhlo's sons were making fun of him by calling angaliyat. Through this incident, one can get to know the casteist mindset of the Patels.

The caste problem starts with the Vankarva voicing out for his community girl when she is being humiliated by the upper caste Patels. And the vengeance remained in all walks of their life. Patel's calm down only after the brutal murder of the Teeho. But still, the discrimination is always seen throughout the novel.

3.2 Sharankumar Limbale's Hindu

Hindu (2010) is a Marathi novel written by Sharankumar Limbale and it was later translated into English by Arun Prabha Mukherjee in 2010. The Caste discrimination in *Hindu* is depicted clearly through politics. This novel *Hindu* seeks to highlight the power politics and further consequences that lead to the killing of a Dalit youth, raping of a Dalit woman and further legal operations from both the caste Hindus and the Dalits is depicted. Tanveen Kaur (2014) states Sharankumar Limbale's Marathi novel, Hindu (2005) is the writer's endeavour to advance the politics of "collectivity" among the politically conscious sections of the democratic country, for studying history as an important vehicle of the past that would help them anticipate a more desired future, only by critically analysing the contemporary present of the casteist/secular India. The text is also the writer's manner to perform the duty of a social doctor and dress the open wounds of the society. It is, at the same time, extending and sharing this task of responsibility with those "assumed readers" who may be affected by the chaotic atmosphere of their society. In this novel, Hindu Kasbe tells that there is a talk about Prabhakar Kamble becoming the next Patil, the head man of the village. As Rambhau Kamble will retire in two years then "Tatya Kamble will get a chance as the post will be reserved for Dalit candidates as by law". (H 4) But Rambhau Kavale will never step down the village headship which his family has enjoyed. He will make sure that his son becomes the next Patil. The upper caste men always want to have the power and politics in order to enjoy the dignity and dominance to subdue the lower caste people under control. In this novel, we can see the power politics between the Kavale and Kamble the group of people in Maharashtra wherein the upper caste men can't tolerate the growth of a Dalit which leads to murder him.

The novel opens with the sound murder of the Dalits by the upper caste men just for the sake of enjoying the political power and the novel ends with a Dalit murdering the upper caste men. Limbale has framed the plot in such a way that no one can escape from the inequality and disfigurement of the caste system. The novel is being narrated by Miland a Dalit seated in the car with upper caste men Gopichand and Manikchand to enjoy the night. The car crossed Bhimnagar decorated with buntings and banner. Suddenly the headlight of the car showed the agitated crowd and 'Murder' shouted Manikchand. Tatya Kamble's blood-soaked body was twitching by the roadside get the car moving shouted Manikchand. Limbale traces the murder of a Dalit as the upper caste men for one reason or the other have the rage to put an end to a Dalit life who is gaining popularity. Every now and then in Daily news and in the history there are many atrocities and murder against the Dalits. Tatya Kamble was giving a speech to the Mahar community exhorting them to convert to escape the curse of untouchability on October 14th in the Dhammachakra Parivartan celebration. Prabhakar Kavale, Gunvant Patil, Jagannath Pandit, Balshetwar were hiding and they came running out with weapons in their hands and pounced upon Tatya Kamble. But somehow he got out of their clutches but Shankar Pujari grabbed him as he started to scream the village doors began to close one after the other, Prabhakar had a sword, Gunvant had a spear, Jagannath Pandit an axe and others had a knife. At that precise moment, Manikchand and Gopichand car arrived on the scene and the violent crowd dispersed. Tatya Kamble fell on the ground. The crowd broke out and they were scattered in different places. Manikchand car came near the gate of Rambhau and told that he saw his son murdering Tatya Kamble. And they made a secret dealing not to reveal it to anyone and dined together for the night. The upper caste men in order to get anything in life they make use of the Dalit life, Dalit women to enjoy their own freedom and luxury of life.

Limbale through Miland portrays the enmity and weakness within the community of Dalits. As the opening of the novel Miland a Dalit is seen enjoying the partnership of the upper caste people Manikchand and Gopichand and they claims that we did good deeds in our past life so now we want to sin by enjoying women and liquor. Gopichand teased Miland by saying that "You must have sinned in your past life. That's why you were born a Mahar." (H 7) Miland fails to question and voice out for the murder and rape of his own community men and women and he never comes forward, to tell the truth, or give witness. His wife Lakshmi tells Miland that "You have sold yourself and want to sell Babasaheb as well." (H xx) In the end of the novel Miland is seen with Gopichand and Manikchand as Limbale puts forth that due to self-loathing his fear he is being metamorphosed as women because of his fear he has lost his manhood. Through this character, Limbale portrays the internal conflict and enemy within the community when he fails to be the part of the movement.

Limbale gives the reason for the murder of a Dalit as Madhukar Kavale was upset because he feared that Tatya Kamble would become the next Patil. Vishnu Pujari felt that people were losing eternal faith as they were going to see jalsa and the collection of the money in the temple were becoming low and Jagannath Pandit felt that because of Tatya Kamble only he lost his job. All of them were unhappy with Tatya Kamble for one reason or other. Tatya Kamble gave a speech about Ambedkar by quoting his words:

> Why do you stay in a religion that does not allow you to enter the temple? Why do you stay in a religion that does not acknowledge your Humanity? Why do you stay in a religion that does not allow you even water? A religion that forbids the treatment of human as the human is not a religion but naked domination. A religion in which touching of unclean animal is permitted but touching of human is prohibited is not a religion but insanity. (H 50, 51)

In another incident, the religious discrimination of the Dalits is being depicted where Dalits now converted to Buddhism. They had thrown away the idols of the Hindu gods and goddesses on to the garbage. Dalits were following new faiths and new ways of worship. Miland's house though still of Hindu idols. His wife Lakshmi stealthily worships them. When an activist comes to their home the idols are to be hidden. His living room represents the portraits of Babasaheb and Buddha, and the kitchen belongs to Hindu gods and goddesses.

> Whenever I feel weak and helpless, I stand before the Hindu gods and goddesses with folded hands. And when I am bloated with self-confidence and dreaming of revolution, I go and stand with a bowed head before Babasaheb Ambedkar and Gautama Buddha's figurines. (H 6)

When the upper caste men feast in Kavale's home after the brutal murder of Tatya Kambale by Prabhakar Kavale Miland gets shocked his eyes filled with tears and thought of Tatya Kamble. He was like a lion the killers have erased the identity of the village as 'Jalsakar Tatya Kamble's village' forever. He felt that "This was an attempt to teach a lesson to ordinary Dalits by killing a Dalit. Who was respected for his talents and had made a name for himself. It was the disfigured face of social terrorism. Dalits have been murdered for thousands of years". (H 12) Whenever a Dalit gains fame or attention in the society the upper caste men try to bring him down or murder him without any clue. As the growth of the Dalits will spoil the harmony, the leadership of the upper caste people and through the murder, the upper caste people try to convey the Dalits that whom 48 so ever rebel against the upper caste will have the same fate. By doing so the Dalits who have no strong foundation of life, and their mere survival is by depending on the upper caste will debt their feelings, emotions, respect and dignity for saving their life from the upper caste men.

Manikchand says to Tatya Kamble that "Kavale has removed the thorn called Tatya Kamble. Now he can have his son anointed as Patil said Gopichand". (H 12) Miland felt that now the law is on the Dalit side and the person who murdered him will surely go to jail. But paying the money they will get bail said Manikchand. Then Miland asked himself many questions was he dead or alive? Is he an activist or not a man? How can he be quite for the murder of Tatya Kamble? The car entered the farmhouse. Sadananad Kamble came running to open the gate he works as a watchman. He was Tatya Kamble's brother he was not aware of the murder. He felt like holding him and weeping on his shoulders. But Manikchand strictly said "Miland, we don't know what we witnessed to this event. Remember the three monkeys of Gandhi". (H 16)

Prabhakar Kavale came into the room with blood rage and caught hold of Manikchand legs and asked him not to reveal that he saw him at the murder spot and claimed that for seventy generations Tatya Kamble's family lived off the scraps which they discharged. But he did not respect our charity. The words of Prabhakar Kavale struck Miland and he felt that "Muslims don't kill Dalits, nor do Christians. Buddhist doesn't commit atrocities on Dalit, nor do Sikhs. Then why do Hindus torment Dalits? Don't they accept the Dalits are Hindu too?" (H 27) Rohit Kamble the son of Tatya Kamble lit the pyre. Tatya Kamble body turned to ashes in a moment. There was a total silence.

The law was in favour of the people. The police visited Kavale's Bara and everyone was nervous. Then constable Marathe asked Rambhau Kavale about Prabhakar but he told that he was in Pune. And the police told them that he was caught and kept in the prison. And police confiscated the sword hidden in the Bara. Constable Marathe and Gautama Gangurde laid a clever trap and caught Jagannath Pandit at his farm for the first time people responsible for committing reckless atrocities against Dalits were behind bars. Madhukar Kavale the elder son of Rambhuva Kavale got a bad dream that that a police dog came to the Bara and sniffed the culprit and it came near Madhukar and he started shouting that he was not the culprit he was an anti-Dalit and he can go and eat in Dalits houses and he can even walk on their street. Then the police took him to Dalit basti. People were shocked to see him on the roads and he woke up very frightened. Then he went to meet Manikchand and Gopichand and the secret talk began to solve the issue. He said that if Sadananad becomes the next Patil then every problem will be solved and in order to make him as a village Patil, they frame a sum of 10 lakh rupees. Then Madhukar Kavale gives him 1 lakh to start the process. The upper caste men make use of money to bring things under control in order to find a temporary solution to the problem Madhukar lines the pocket of Manikchand and Gopichand. In due course, both made use of the money for their personal purpose and it never reached the Dalits.

The dominance of the upper caste people in education is seen clearly in the novel. The school reopened Kasbe Guruji was teaching a lesson on Babasaheb Ambedkar. The news spread in the village, Narendra Patil and other people went to the school and they tore the pages of that book. Kasbe Guruji applied for a transfer and felt that it was a casteist village as he felt unsafe there. Godbole Guruji and Kasbe Guruji were engaged in a heated discussion that not all Hindus are casteist. Hindu religion is a tolerant religion too. Then Kasbe told him that "you are right. We should consider the cow holy and the untouchable unholy. Offer milk to the poisonous snake and murder the untouchable. Is this what you call tolerance?"(H 36)

The upper caste people feel that even the sight and touch of the Dalits are impure. Every walk of the life a Dalits faces discrimination. Limbale through the character Sonali gives a sketch of the upper caste women who tries to cross the traditional boundaries to attire her dreams but is anchored by the castiest father. Ever since Sonali came to Achalpur, as a new bride, she was enchanted by the sound of dholaki drums. She was married to Prabhakar and she heard the drums and went upstairs to see the dance, her heart ached thinking of the sweet and sour memories of her happy college days. She was given a dance recital at the annual function and that gained a lot of fame for her and the local papers published her photographs and interviews and along her side, in the paper, there were Rohit Tatya Kamble's son, a Dalit boy she even praised him and it created anger with the savarnas. She and Rohit got to know each other only in the dance and they became close friends. While the savarnas boys sent the photograph of Rohit and Sonali dance together to her father. As soon as Baliram Patil saw it he felt angry. Sonali had the habit of writing poems and many got published too and when Sonali's dairy of poems got into her father's hand he mistook it and put an end to Sonalis education.

After the murder slowly the situation gained momentum by the construction of new houses for the Dalits and Kabir Kamble felt that everyone should convert their religion from Hindu to Buddhism. But the idea turned him very somber "We have depended on the savarnas for our daily bread even after conversion. Our God will change, our rituals of worship will change but the question regarding dal roti won't change. A complete transformation is not possible until the economic slavery of the Dalits is washed away.

Kabir Kamble tells Rohit Kamble the son of Tatya Kamble that it is hard to fight the social orders with weapons because the enemy is hiding in the scriptures. And Rohit Kamble replied him by saying "you can use a weapon to murder, but not to bring about change. The savarnas too are victims of the caste system. Their casteist mindset is thousand years old. We will have to fight against them deeply ingrained beliefs." (H-102) Sadananad became the next Patil of the village with the help of Gopichand and Manikchand. The people in the village was very much disturbed that the independence day will fall on the next week and the village sarpanch has to hoist the flag and distribute the sweets and the villagers did not like a Dalit doing such things. Narendra Patil and Sadananad Kamble had arguments before the panchayat meeting. He threatened him that he will sit on the sarpanch chair and never let him. For which Sadananad protested and Narendra Patil took his chappals and started beating Sadananad in front of everyone. And the next two days newspaper carried about this news.

Manikchand and Gopichand sat with Sadananad Kamble at their farmhouse. Sadananad was greatly perturbed by the beating and thrashing as of which was a challenge to the twin brothers. This instigated him by saying the villagers have killed your brothers and now they have used chappals to beat you. Only the weapons are different and he said that he has to change the style of the fight rather than the weapons. Gopichand advised Sadananad not to take any steps against the incident and he told him to support the Hindus so that he can become the MLA Dalits votes alone won't help him. In order to gain the villagers votes he had to support even the killers of Tatya Kamble.

Later on after series of incidents Manikchand, Gopichand and Sadananad went in the car and they reached Hema Pandit's house and they spoke to the people over there and Manikchand tells them that Sadananad is our man and we are planning for him to contest the Assembly election next time and we want your support. Sadananad Kamble got the minister post and Achalpur celebrated his victory. A grand pooja was performed in the temple. After some years many people were on their way to the city to hear the judgment. The court compound was crowded. The Dalit activists were present in large number to hear the judgment. The law supported the villagers and Kavale's families were happily waiting to see Prabhakar Kavale. The parade was nearing the Bara. Prabhakar Kavale was puffed with pride. Sonali stood to face Prabhakar, performing arti. Suddenly people saw Prabhakar Kavale's body fall on the ground. It was Kabir Kamble who rained his bullets at Prabhakar Kavale. And Prabhakar Kavale is dead. Thus, the rivalry ends in the novel by the common man murdering the upper caste men.

3.3. G. Kalyan Rao's Untouchable Spring

Untouchable Spring (2000) was written in Telugu and later it was translated into English by…In this novel, G. Kalyan Rao reveals the sufferings and pains of the Dalits with seven generations of history. T Joseph R Jayakar (2014) states that in the story behind the story of *Antarani Vasantam* (*Untouchable Spring*) the author talks about the grim state of Dalits (Untouchables) in India. The novel is timely narrating the incidents through Ruth. Ruth was a nurse and Reuben was the hospital's pastor. "The past recedes. The present is before her. If we build a nest and perch in the past that has gone by, the present too will become the past. But Ruth says her memory does not relate to the past. She says Reuben is always her present". (US 1) As silently as Reuben came into her life, he just left as silently. He left his innumerable springs all through her life and left. He told many stories and poems. He told his stories on a moonlit night he used to tell the stories over and over again "He laughed as he narrated. Cried as he narrated. His eyes sparkle then. His eyes got wet then. She smeared that 'wetness' on her eyelids. In truth, they are not just the memories he shared. Wet eyes wrench the heart. Touch the spinal cord. They haunt". (US 1) He and his ancestral swam in the savage of flood water and some were washed away. Reuben was a beautiful untouchable man these words may sound strange but Ruth used this words simply and naturally "She used to speak those words to Reuben himself. 'Oh, my beautiful untouchable man!' She would call him like that innumerable times". (US 2)

The way in which the caste discrimination originated is portrayed through Reuben's narration of his ancestral story to her. He says about the Kamadhenu, it was a special cow which gave the milk and it tasted as honey only the gods and goddesses were allowed to drink the milk. Chennaiah who takes care of the cow wants to taste the milk, he tells about his wish to Parvati. She advises him to ask Kamadhenu about tasting its milk and when he asks about it to Kamadhenu it falls and dies on the spot when the gods come to know about it they wanted to cut the meat and taste it but it should be done on one condition that the cow has to be shifted to another place and then it had to be cut so they call Jambavanta to replace the cow he does it and they ask him to cook the meat but they advise him to cut the cow into two half so that one half can be cooked and the other will be allowed to turn into life by Rishis. But they cooked the whole meat and one piece fell down but Chennaiah took the piece and again put it into the cooked food and gods cursed them saying that in Kaliyuga Jambavanta's children become *Madigas* and Chennaiah's children become *Malas*. He completed the story saying that my Grandfather told this and it is the story of my birth and your birth and the curse of the wrath of gods. Malas and Madigas are the Dalit.

The socio-cultural aspects of the Dalits and the way of living is portrayed in the novel. Yellena Dinni that was where Reuben's father Yellanna was born he grew up sang songs and danced. Yellanna did not write songs he knew no alphabet. "All he had was a feeling heart, a sharable experience, tear-shedding eyes, swelling nerve, a turbulent blood-stream… that was it, the song would weave itself". (US 6) They called him singing Yelladu, dancing Yelladu but his father's sister Boodevi called him Yellanna. When Yellanna sings the moving tune that combined untouchability and hunger would be heard. The place where those who belonged to the four castes lived was *ooru.* The place where Malas lived–*Malapalli,* where the Madigas lived-*Madigapalli* and all these parts put together formed Yennela Dinni.

Yellanna was born like everyone. "Oh, you upper caste people! I, an untouchable, am walking on your pure, regal paths. Move aside. Move aside". (US 7) He announced his birth like anyone else. Like each one's birth touching one father's heart, his too, touched his father's heart. 'A male', he shouted out to the caste elder. He filled with caste elder's stomach with toddy and felt elated. When *Yerra gollalu* came to the *ooru* there was excitement all over because they would put up street plays for ten to fifteen days in a row. Boodevi was crazy for *Chenchu Natakam* she would go to play taking her nephew along. Karanams and Kapus would sit close to the performers. Behind them, people from the washerman, barber and potter castes would sit. The Malas would sit on the mala mound. The Madigas would sit on the madiga mound. Those two groups would be far away from the arena. Sitting like that they would not be visible to the village elders and the elders of the other caste. The play would not begin till the Karanam and Kapus arrived. After they arrived they would praise him to skies. Then the *sutradhara* would begin the performance. Yellanna would say to his aunt that he cannot see the play she would get up and lift him and if the Karanam and Kapus see her standing that would be in trouble. But she dares to stand for her nephew because of the play he would sacrifice his sleep. He asked his aunt that can he sit near the yerra gollalu but she refused in spite of her refusal. Yellanna went near the performing stage and he stood and after some time he found some people staring at him. When they came to know he was from mala they started attacking him they pelted stones on him he ran for his life. He jumped into the water and reached the shore and only then he knew that there was no waist cloth he started walking on the path. He waited till the dark and then he walked for sure that no one would have seen him.

A mala or madiga could not live in Yennela Dinni without doing bonded labour. The life of Yennela Dinni was all under the elder Karanam's surveillance. Most of the Yennela Dinni lands were in the hands of Karanam. Very little was in the hands of other castes. The Reddy's had some land but they were just under tenants the other caste had a cent or kunta, malas and madigas had no land. When the first rain came the higher ups among the Karanam servant would come to malapalli and madigapalli. One per family has to come and help them plough fields the whole week they would do the ploughing. The wages would be afternoon lunch and no money would be given. Though they would call one for a family but the whole family would come to work. While providing meals the malas and madigas would fight among themselves stating the food was given more to other person than them. They would even fight for leftover grains on the floor. “Using the malas to beat up the madigas and the madigas to beat up the malas, the karanam would bloster their pride, saying each of their castes was great. They would fight hard”. (US 29) The malapalli and madigapalli were in the threshold of danger in Yennela Dinni they were near the stream and if there was flood water would come first to those palles. Many times they thought of raising the level of two palles. “The upper caste would not tolerate the untouchables living on a higher plane. They would say that the malas and madigas ought always to live in the lower regions. If they lived on a higher plane, the arrogance of the upper caste would not tolerate it”. (US 30)

In Yennela Dinni these wretched people’s lives remained mere desire. They were distraught and ruined due to their desires. It just happened with father Narigadu. There were heavy rain and continuous storm in the place mala and madigas would almost be covered by water it was at the time the people gathered and talked about going to mound where upper caste people lived. The father took Naganna on his hip and mother placed the basket on her hand. “If you want to live, come along. Whoever comes in the way will be the targets of this axe… those who want to live, come along… we’ll die anyway… Yellamma too has been submerged. Come, come, you coward bastards… come on, you…” (US 32) The people started following him. “For the first time, the untouchable storm fell on the ooru. For the first time in the Yellena Dinni, so many malas and madigas were walking amidst houses of the upper caste, on their paths, in the middle of the ooru, crossing the lanes of the temple… walking towards the mound”. (US 32) They were on top of the mound at a higher level than upper caste. They had confidence that they will not die. In the morning it appeared as if malapalli and madigapalli were washed away. Whatever they carried they cooked and they ate. The water has wiped out malapalli and madigapalli. That day no one had food to eat it was getting dark father was missing and in the night the four people came on the heads with bags full of rice they broke the sahukar’s shop and now people would gather and they would be talking only about us. They started cooking the rice and they ate greedily. The people spoke

"They tell us not to live on heights. The stream tells us not to live in low-lying areas. If we come to the top, they'll kill us. If we are in the lower areas, the stream will kill us. No matter what, death is inescapable. But … listen…listen to our words. We aren't born only to die". (US 35) Naganna could not sleep he was awake listening to the conversations of the elders. The next day it was normal nothing happened but in the evening the people carried a corpse and it was the death of his father.

The novel portrays how the Dalits worked as a bonded labourer for the upper caste. One day in the late evening elder Karanam went into the eastern part of the field. Only Atchireddy's mother Rangayi would sit under the banyan tree and wait for the elder Karanam to be killed. When Subbireddi and Rangayi came to sell their cattle in the market and get money for their living it was Karanman who saw Subbireddi and asked him to work with him from then on he worked under him and whatever money he gets he gives to elder Karanam to maintain the accounts. Rangayi felt that she should go to the native place so she asked Subbireddi to clear the account and take the money with him but when he went and asked to Karanam about the accounts he got angry and so far no one dared to ask him about the money and the accounts. Karanam sent Subbireddi and asked him to come some other day. The next day Subbireddi was found dead in the cattle shed as people reported it was due to snake-bite but Rangayi found that he was strangled in the neck to death as she found the dark lines in his neck but she could not say it out to anybody. From then she waited for elder karanam to be killed. That was the day when elder karanam came to the field and his head was chopped by madiga Mataiah. Rangayi was the witness it was dark everywhere only Rangayi and Banyan tree was still and silent. "He killed Narigadu. He died in my hand now". (US 54)

Ruth remembers Reuben's words that years passed by kings died kingdoms collapsed the white men crossed the oceans but "Wonder. Nothing was destroyed. Caste, untouchability, criminal acts, looting-nothing ended. In fact, those who said everything was in the Vedas began seeing white men's feet". (US 63) Naganna thought all the things which Chandrappa had thought to him. It took three months for him and the other artist to learn the dance and drama and one day they started to enact on the stage. Enacting in the stage gave them fame and but the problem came when the enactors has to ask before the play whether the karanam has come but when Naganna and Yellanna performed they never asked but they said "Have the great 'pedda mala' and the 'pedda madiga' who is as great has come?". (US 79) The way the people reacted irritated the karanams and it became a major issue. It was a shame for them when the people reacted like this and they could not digest that change. "In their eyes, Naganna and Yellanna appeared like big criminals. They thought they ought not to swallow the heinous act of raising the mala and madiga to the level of a karanam or a kapu. They thought of teaching them both a lesson". (US 79)

When Atchireddy's father-in-law came to visit his daughter he heard the karanam and Atchireddy talking about Atelladu. He said after listening to everything "If it were me, I would kill those two bastards". (US 79) When he knew that there was a performance in his place Dibbalamitta he sent word to a man of what must be done. Bukkireddy sent word to the mala and madigas elders the day before the performance. He told that "if Atelladu's performance took place in Dibbalamitta both the palles would be reduced to ashes". (US 80) If they want to perform they should not call the pedda mala and the pedda madinga the way the karanams and kapus were called. Naganna found it strange and felt that the life was taking him on a different direction. He sent a word to Polayi and Mataiah's nephew Musalaiah. All gathered and they planned to make the mala mound cultivable as the karanam's used the land for bonded labour they even occupied devadasis land so these people started clearing the land of the mala only after the third day the elders in the ooru arranged the meeting karanam and Atchireddy and the other reddys gathered and when the issue was put up Naganna came forward to tell that it was he who did it and he thought to tell it to karanam when the work was over. This time in the meeting karanam found much difference in the way the people talked. The meeting ended as the karanam got up and said "Families shouldn't sit on our heads. But they aren't clearing up the mala's mound for families to live, right?" (US 87) The malas and madigas made the malas mound cultivable. They shared the piece of land with each other. They ought to remember Narigadu and Mataiah. Their sacrifice, courage, the blood they shed and the history continued like that. The karanam did not consider much for the mala's land but it irritated him.

The day for the performance in Dibbalamitta was nearing and they were cautious that the people from different places came toward Dibbalamitta in order to support the karanams and Reddys. Naganna felt why should he perform in the ooru by representing everyone and told that he was not a cattle in their shed to do what he wishes? The day of the performance came and it was a dilemma whether to address the gathering or to perform. "The palles did not dare have a performance addressing the elders with respect. Doing such a thing needed a lot of courage. Therefore, Yellanna thought not to perform would be the best way to save self-respect". (US 89) Yellanna said to the people that let's not perform now let's do it on another time. That day the walk to Yennela Dinni was very heavy. It was a great defeat to Naganna he never spoke a word. In the night he sang the song and Yellanna were with him after some time he told that he felt sleepy and he closed the eyes and he never opened the eyes again.

During when potter Pedakoteswarudu started writing dvipada poems alongside making pots everyone appreciated his posts, not poems because what the Brahmins speaks alone is the Veda. Whatever it is it has to be spoken only by them but when Brown started collecting the works of Vemana the Brahmins encouraged it. Potter Pedakoteswarudu did not like this and gave up his caste he started saying Brahmin, reddy, potter, washerman, mala, barber, madiga everyone was mud. He wrote his Vedanta pundits made fun of it. He made Vinayaka with mud and pundits did pooja for it, he started mingling with everyone he would go to the houses of mallapalli. He would eat whatever was served to him. He would drink sour gruel from madigapalli. One day he crossed the Brahmin bazaar to see Mala bairagi the people of the upper caste spoke badly of him and asked him to go away and they threw the mud on away on which he walked so potter Koteswarudu spitted on the mud and asked them to throw away the mud by taking it in their hands. The Brahmins felt that he has insulted him. He met Mala bairagi and he was looking at him in amazement. He said to him that the white man is putting on paper all the verses which were on palm-leaf. So let's light the fire and start to write and he put the verses about Subhadra, Yennela Dinni, Naganna, Narigadu and Mataiah. When Koteswarudu asked to tell his name he told Yellanna Atalelladu. Patalelladu Yellanna said that "Song was born in my house. Dance learns its beat from my life. That's why, no matter how far they flung me, they only ran towards my house. They were born with me and will become dust with me". (US 103) In the night they slept together and morning he took the palm leafs and walked towards the end of the Ooru and bid farewell and went the upper caste people attacked him and burnt the palm leaves and before Yellanna could come there he Koteswarudu was in the pool of blood and he bid his last farewell by saying "I'm going Basavudu" Yellanna lit the pyre and he did not know who is Basavudu even Naganna haven't told him about it and he heard it much time from Koteswarudu.

The water would be first irrigated to the Karanams and then to the Reddys and then the potters, washer man and then finally to the malas and madigas. The water was irrigated but when the water reached Atchireddy's field he gave the lame excuse that if the water is sent to mala and madiga then the pathway would be with water and the Reddys cart cannot go on the roadway so he did not allow water for irrigation. That night Pittodu, Poladu, Musalaiah and Mallaiah planned to divert the water from Atchireddy's field and they made their plan success. Everyone in the village was surprised but Atchireddy caught hold of the four people and harmed them badly at that time Subhadra took the spade in her hand and went towards the field of Atchireddy and broke the canal and the water started gushing out and the people thought she was possessed by some goddess. People believed that it was a goddess in her because a normal untouchable girl would not be able to do such things.

> Sivaiah thought that where ever he go the people hurt him badly:
>
> Humans too. Brains too.
> In Tamil country, Pariah
> In Kannada country,'hooleelu.

> In Maharashtra, mangs, mahars, bhangis and chamars.
> Among Telugus, mala and madigas.
> Like this in many places and in every corner of the country. (US 144)

The people got changing to Christianity and this irritated the Hindu people and they started burning the Bible and hurting the people who worshipped Christ. "Attack! On the mala people. On the madiga people. Attack. On mala Christ. Attack. On the madiga Christ. It would be enough if Christ were untouchable. There would certainly be an attack". (US 170) Martin and Simon gave preaching in the town about Christ. They came to know that some land was barren they approached Karanam to ask for it but he told it was not barren land he refused to give but he approached the white man and told the situation and he took some people and sat in front of the white man's house and later he got the land and gave it to the poor farmers.

The Christmas came they discussed to name the child and many people came and attacked Martin and they stabbed him and they attacked him and they left the place. Simon took Martin on his shoulder to save him but it was of no use. The upper caste people started to attack the mala and madiga. Many were killed, the huts were burning the smoke from the flame touched the sky. Saramma and Sasirekha turned to corpse then Simon took the child and he thought to save the child at that child is Reuben. Ruth cried whenever she remembered the scene:

> In this country the air one breathes has caste.
> The water one drinks have caste.
> The field canal that flows and the land that yields harvest have caste.
> The school, the temple, and the village square have caste.
> The food one eats the house one lives in and the clothes one wears have caste.
> The word one speaks has caste.
> Literature and culture have caste.
> The state has caste, its law has caste.

> Justice and the court have caste.
> The corpse and the cemetery have caste.
> God has caste. Devil has caste. (US 227)

The casteism is seen evident in the novel no matter where the Dalits live but they always face discrimination in that place from other caste people. In the ancient days the caste discrimination was seen directly but as the days goes by the discrimination is seen indirectly in the society. Always the upper caste authors and the Dalit writers portray about the exclusion of the Dalits in the society but when there will be a change to really accept Dalits as a part of the community which will lead to inclusion. The change has to come in the minds of the caste Hindus to shed the discrimination and adopt equality within Human.

3.4 Kancha Ilaiah's Untouchable God

Untouchable God (2013) written by Kancha Ilaiah is the novel from Telangana written directly in English in the year 2013. In this novel Paraiah, a Dalit is apparently beaten to death while walking about his village in the evening, allegedly for the crime of thinking about God, which might well lead to thoughts of equality. Six Brahmin men Veda Shastry, Namboodri, Krishnamurthy, Appa Rao, Tilak and Banerjee celebrate the death of a Dalit.

In *Untouchable God* (2013), the caste discrimination can be seen evidently practiced by the upper caste Brahmins considering the dalits as inferior and dependent to them. The Paraiah were the working class they have to work day and night without rest. They are squeezed till the last blood in their body. Paraiah had worked all day collecting the grains cut by women and bundling it so they could carry it away. Only an exceptional man like Paraiah did both male and female tasks:

> Yet in the life of Paraiah no pleasures seem to exist. All the really important things he did, like killing the chicken or bundling the corps, were for others, not for him or his children. The only pleasure he tasted was that of feeding the corps with water and manure, and feeding his master's cattle. These acts marked him as a sinner, while his master, who owned both crops and cattle, but fed neither, was pure. The only truly pure thing, it seemed to

> him, was eating. The landlord ate for the benefit of the village, and the priest ate for the benefit of Gods. (UG 4)

Paraiah felt sad because he suffered the endless pain that came when a human being was forced to lead the life of a dog. The Hindu gods had failed to impress the divine separateness of caste on these dogs. The Brahmins lived on the other side of the village, far from this street. They lived in their divine feudal lands called Agraharas. "The gods gave them lands so they could stay away from the productive humans, socially connecting dogs and beasts of burden called donkeys". (UG 5-6) The Hindu gods have not stooped to create Chandalas, Paraiahs or dogs, therefore, the Brahmins hated them most. The Brahmins hated these things more than shit. The Brahmins felt that "God created the Brahmins from his head, the Kshatriyas from his shoulders, the Vaishyas from his thighs and the Shudras from his feet. The Panchamas- the filth were unborn". (UG 18) The Panchamas, of whom Paraiah was one, were never created by God.

Kancha Ilaiah puts forth in this novel shows how a Brahmin makes use of the lower caste girl just to have sex in the name of sambandham without marrying her. The lower caste people are considered to be polluted, untouchable, non-cultured but when it comes to sex everything fades away. The touch of lower caste men is considered to be impure but the body is exempted for sex. Namboodri was travelling in bus. He was distracted by the man who sat beside him and some of his parts touched Namboodri. He felt that "Evil days: A Brahmin gets touched so casually by an unknown, perhaps an untouchable! These buses are profane places". (UG 23) When the upper caste men need a woman they would get over it from the lower caste family. Namboodri was twenty he went to Govinda Nair's house and he spoke to him and he proposed his wish for marrying his daughter Sita Mahalaxmi. With this happy news, he went to tell to his wife but his wife was weeping and said,

> My hopes are crumbled. Do you really wish her to live in sambandham? With all the namelessness my life is better: she will have neither face nor name. She will be the mother of Brahmin children but shall remain an unwed Nair. Can her children become

> Brahmins, let alone Namboodris? Can they become priests in any temple? You foolish man, how could you agree? (UG 28).

Sita's mother disagrees to give to Brahmins but Govindan Nair roared "A Brahmin- Namboodri- is a God of gods on Earth. Whatever they ask, they ask only to increase our virtue. Our Gods said that whatever a Brahmin asks, you must give it whether it be wealth, cattle or daughter". (UG 29) Govindan Nair said that as a spiritual demand he will give his daughter only to Namboodris and no one can stop it.

While the Brahmin justified whatever they did was right either it is food, women, work or sex. "A Brahmin enters into the sexual act, not for the appetites of his physical body but for the pleasure of God, while the Shudras, the untouchables, the tribals- the undivine archaic people- enter into the act only to have their own selfish bodily pleasure". (UG 30) So they were not considered to be divine. Hence the sons born to those castes do not have the power to send the father's soul to heaven. This was the reason why they remained Shudras, Chandalas and tribals. Aryavartha was the only country where the Gods exalted the spiritual sex. He was reminded of the Rig Veda which contained slokas after slokas about how Indra, the God of gods have loved women- not his wife of course- the apsara, divine prostitute created by gods to satisfy their own pleasure. "Occasionally he regretted that he had to perform his researchers with such low material". (UG 35)

The discrimination is even experienced in terms of education as it is always the rule that the educated Brahmin wants the Shudras to be away from knowledge the Shudras should not even aspire or think about attaining wisdom. When Balaram a Dalit saw the priest sitting in the temple and teaching four children he approached the priest and asked for his daughter's education and the priest asked him which caste he belonged to and when he said he was Shudra the priest said:

> I am a pundit and priest of this temple. Above all, I am a Brahmin. Do you think we teach Shudras, Chandalas, dogs and donkeys? Who let you march into the temple like this and ask me whether I would teach you low-born daughter a girl, a damned bitch puppy! Get out! Out of this temple! Take your defiling feet off my floor!. (UG 69)

Another incident in the novel through the character of Mala shows how education can be a hindrance for a girl to get her dreams come true. Mala tells to Isaiah when he visits India how her Parents accepted her to do Ph.D. only when she came forward to go with the wish of her parents to marry whomever they show as the bridegroom. She even explains the state of other women how even the present generation girls didn't even learn their letters. "Till recently it was believed that if a girl tempted the fates, such as by learning to read, she would cause her husband's death". (UG 238)

Religious discrimination is the root cause for all the other discrimination as the Gods of Hindus are considered to be the heavenly and cultured and the Gods of the Shudras are of less power and untouched. The nine days of Ganesh was brought into the street. The Shudras distributed the Pamphlet. Some Paraiah came running to see the deity. Shudras stopped them and said "Don't come in here, you Paraiah Ganesh is a Hindu God. Not an Untouchable God". (UG 97) Tilak came with his followers and said Ganesh will visit the Shudra street too. The Paraiah men shouted "We too have bodies. Are they not created by Gods? When the sound of our drums is touchable for God why not our bodies?" (UG 97) After the festival Tilak invited all the people and told the tolerance behind the plan he told them briefly that one of the Brahmin is being arrested by the police and the Muslims are high in number we have to stimulate the lower caste Shudras and tell them that the Muslim men attacked their men in the marketplace and if the rivalry between them broke out our Brahmin would be released and the investigation will turn upon the Shudras. He asked the people to heat the Shudras with passion and righteousness. "No Brahmin boy should go to jail". (UG 91) Doing such incident the Brahmin gained the religious bonding and made the Shudras subdue for the knowledge they possess and brought out a rift between other religions.

When Isaiah came to India to know about the caste and the problems faced by the Dalit people he asked his doubt about their semi-naked status they are like Gandhi did Gandhi also beg. For which Jacob said "There was a man called Manu many centuries ago, who wrote a book saying that lower-caste women should always offer themselves to the gaze of the upper-caste men. If they cover themselves, they will be assaulted and punished". (UG 183) He further said that Manu also said that Dalit should not own property, gold or ornament. They have to cook only in a broken pot and eat in mutilated bowls. Elumalai narrated how the upper caste men made use of the lower caste women while saying this his eyes became red "not from drinking liquor but from drinking history…the history of untouchable slavery…the history of women's untouchable bodies and touchable private parts". (UG 192) Elumalai, Jacob, and Isaiah went to see the Shiva temple the upper caste people started attacking them with stones and Elumalai got hurt. When they saw Isaiah coming they said: "An untouchable with a black devil was coming towards their Gods!" (UG 198) Jacob and Isaiah went to the bookshop to purchase some books he took the book on Rig Veda. He read some words in the book:

> God has made the caste: the Brahmins from his head, the Kshatriyas from his shoulders and arms, the Baniyas from his belly and the Shudras from his feet. The untouchables and women weren't mentioned at all. He remembered the words of Genesis: 'So God created man in his own image. In the image of God created He him, Male and Female created He them.' (UG 212)

Each religious people considered themselves as superior and the others as inferior and they separated the people and enmity were formed and it leads to the extent of murdering the people. The Brahmins lived on the other side of the village, far from this street. They lived in their divine feudal lands called agraharas. "The Gods gave them lands so they could stay away from the productive humans, socially connecting dogs and beasts of burden called donkeys". (UG 5-6) The Hindu Gods has not stooped to create Chandalas, Paraiahs or dogs, therefore, the Brahmins hated them most. Paraiah felt the pain in him for being untouchable,

> Why then had the Gods allowed him to be born? If the Gods had nothing to do with it, maybe there were other Gods, enemies of the High Gods and creators of the fallen. But if so, where were these others? Why weren't they doing their jobs? The High Gods gave their followers land, grain, money, and status. If Paraiah's

> life was the gift of the other Gods, he would have liked to be able, just one, to tell them what he thought of them. (UG 7-8)

When the lower caste people tried to be cultured and civilised the sight of it also cannot be tolerated by the upper caste people. Namboodri on the way in the bus he saw people wearing shirts and he felt that during his day's people were semi-naked. In this country where humidity and heat are prevailed it is good to see people half dressed and he felt that when he was a child in 1880's men and women wore the only mundu. Kerala women never wore blouses. Prophet Mohammed said to Arabs to come to Allah's mosque only with fully covered bodies wearing switched clothes from toe to head. Women wearing switched burkhas had come to spoil the women of Kerala. He felt how wearing clothes could be the end of all modesty. And when the Christian hospital people were giving treatment to the Paraiyar the upper caste people hated them and spoke ill of their religion. He was distracted by the man who sat beside him and some of his parts touched Namboodri. He felt that "Evil days: A Brahmin gets touched so casually by an unknown, perhaps an untouchable! These buses are profane places". (UG-23) But the person was dressed well if he was untouchable he would be smelt fishy and meaty so Namboodri asked his name he said Matthew, Namboodri snuffed "A Christian! This bloody Matthew could be of any caste! The Christians and Muslims in Kerala would definitely go to hell for spoiling the sanctity of God's own country". (UG 23)

The Brahmins in Kerala didn't like the Christians as they were converting all the Dalits to Christianity and giving education for the Dalits and making them cultured and Civilised as British were spreading Christianity. Kerala is going Christian; going Christian was the household refrain of Brahmin families. In Kerala, the Ezhavas who were toddy tappers were revolting under the leadership of Narayana Guru. Namboodri called for the Meeting of the temple there were eight members and a British official. He saw the British officer chair and said this chair of Christian has to be removed. He ordered to remove the chair of the British beef eating Christian. Namboodri said "British had not only brought bad administration but also a bad God, a God who did not distinguish between Brahmin and Chandala.

Even if they left tomorrow this Untouchable God would stay on here to spoil the air and water of Aryavarta". (UG 48) Namboodri started running toward the church and he went inside and he saw the Jesus statue and he saw the priest speaking to the people of what God has told but Namboodri felt how can a God speak in prose to people directly, his mind was in a whirl. He wants to live as a Christian Namboodri said to his Sister-in-law. "But I do not wish to be, I cannot be, a Christian among untouchables. I cannot imagine that God is untouchable too. Can you find out if there is a Brahmin Christian anywhere in this God's own country or outside it?" (UG 53)

Kancha Ilaiah (2013) states in this novel how a religious discrimination can go to the extent of murdering the fellow human. The brutality of the man in the name of religion is clearly depicted in this novel. Hussein and Saraswathi studied together in the school and love blossomed between them. Their parents accepted and Nikah was arranged Saraswati's name changed to Mumtaj Bee and she went to her in-law's house. "A mosque education was followed by a mosque marriage and a mosque name. And a Hindu Saraswathi became a Muslim Mumtaj Bee". (UG 78) It was Friday and people gathered for the mosque but they saw Hussien's body in a pool of blood one eye socket empty and his private parts were cut and his chest was crushed and there was a note "ANY CUTORGAN DARES TO MARRY A HINDU GIRL THIS WILL BE THE FAIT". (UG 78) Balaram's house was so silent and outside the house hung a banner "IF MUMTAJ BEE DO NOT BECOME SARASWATI WITHIN WEEK SHE ALSO FOLLOW HER HUSBAND". (UG 78) Under this someone has scribbled "*Any Shudra lerns letter any were in world will have punishment like Sarwathi call Mumtaj Bee met*". (UG 78) The news of the murder was spread in the newspaper. Many people gathered near the mosque to meet the chairman Yusuf Ali Khan. They discussed the murder and they asked to type a pamphlet about the incident and they asked the people to distribute it after the mosque and then they can take the sword and cut as many heads as possible but women should not be raped. Muslims were planning to kill much more people. "HEAD FOR HEADS...TWO HEADS FOR ONE PRIVATE ORGAN." (UG 84)

The Caste Hindus make use of the situation to bring the Shudra's under control at any circumstance in their life. Tilak invited all the people and told the tolerance behind the plan he told them briefly that one of the Brahmin is being arrested by the police and the Muslims are high in number we have to stimulate the lower caste Shudras and tell them that the Muslim men attacked their men in the marketplace and if the rivalry between them broke out our Brahmin would be released and the investigation will turn upon the Shudras. He asked the people to heat the Shudras with passion and righteousness. "No Brahmin boy should go to jail". (UG 91) The dressing sense of the Christian their food habits were being made fun off. Each religion considers itself to be superior and it people behaved like an animal when it came to religious patriotism.

The Dalits work all day in the field and household of the Brahmins but still their poverty is not abolished and they are treated equally to animals by doing all the odd jobs for the Brahmins without self-respect, dignity, and reputation. Paraiah had worked all day collecting the grains cut by women and bundling it so they could carry it away. Only an exceptional man like Paraiah did both male and female tasks. The Paraiah men have described as:

> He was black as buffalo, his hair was longish and he had no upper garment, only a loincloth around his waist. Of medium height, he had a slight, rather sparse beard. The boniness of his frame was unmitigated by muscle, and his skin, robbed early of its natural tautness, hung in wrinkles. (UG 2)

Weariness bent his limbs like Lord Rama's bow, but his soul appeared heavier. He felt more pain when the landlord asked him to kill a chicken, but he longed to taste the chicken curry but to the end, he would only get only the bones as a reward for the slaughter. The landlord's family would get flesh because they never committed the sin of cutting the bird's throat. "They, the givers of orders and the eaters, were sacred: he, the slayer and the ordered, was not. Sacredness appeared and disappeared like sunshine". (UG 4)

The summer days of Paraiah went on starving and they would feed on the dead cattle which died of airborne disease. The hope of chicken or mutton would go unmet for years and in some families it would go thus for a generation. Paraiah felt sad because "Instead he suffered the endless pain that came when a human being was forced to lead the life of a dog". (UG 4) Paraiah dreamt that his children and the dogs were fighting over the same bones. He did not ever want to see that day in real life. All through the life of a Dalit, the discrimination is being faced and the novel puts forth to the readers by portraying the discrimination in various states of the upper caste Brahmin to the Dalits.

3.5 Bama's Vanmam-vendetta

Bama's "*Vanmam-Vendetta*" [vengeance, revenge] (2008) portrays the animosity between two Dalit sub-castes. D. Sudhakara Rao (2016) states that Bama's Vanmam-Vendetta, which first appeared in Tamil in 2002, is not the usual novel of atrocities against Dalits, though atrocities are depicted, particularly the brutality of the police against women when they cannot vent their rage on the absconding men. But rather than focus on violence, it strikes at the heart of one of the most problematic aspects of Dalit identity: the enmity that frequently exists among different Dalit castes themselves. The protagonists here are two Dalit castes, Parayars and Pallars, in Kandampatti village of Tamil Nadu. Pallars and Parayas are the two Dalit Castes discussed in the text. Pallars remained as the Hindus where as Parayas are seen as Christian converts. The novel deals with how the Naickers, one of the dominant castes in Tamil Nadu stroke the fire between Pallars and Parayas to preserve Naickers own status. Marginalised people, those who have been pushed to the very edges of society, have put aside their internal enmities if they are to reclaim their self-respect and their rightful place in the society.

Kandampatti is a big village. People of many different castes live there. It is surrounded by mountain, whenever the people have no job they used to go to the forested mountain and collect the wood and they would sell it to Thevars, Naickers, and Nadars:

> The Parayars lived in the eastern part of the village. The first of these houses is where Saminathan's family lives. Starting from there, the Parayars occupy four or five streets at the eastern edge.

> Next to them are the four or five streets at the edge. Next to them are the four or five streets of pallar houses. Some distance away from the Parayar and Pallar houses are the Kakkalayar houses. In about four or five streets there are the weaver Chaliyars, the Moopanars, and Pannadis. Near the western bazaar live the Thevars, Chettiars, Aasaris, Pillais, Nadars, Naickers, and so on. (VV 4-5)

The Pallars and Parayars fight among themselves to know their position in the society. As one moves from east to west in the village, the caste status of the residents steadily rises. To the west lie the agricultural fields and they all belong to the upper-caste people. The Parayars are the only Christians here, yet the church is not on any of their streets it is in the western part of the village. The Pallars have their own chavady and it is the place where their village meeting would take place. "Unlike the Parayar's not many of the Pallars leave the village to get an education. They go to school in the village, itself, and drop out midway". (VV 6) During Saminathan grandfather's time they used to be cleaning the landowner's house, and clearing the cow dung. But in his parent's generation, everything has been changed. The Naikers did not want to work on their own farms so they gave it to lease to the Parayars. The Parayars who toiled hard day and night to turn the barren land to fertile land and, according to the season, they sowed the seeds and improved their economic status. But the Pallars did not take farmland on lease or toil in the fields to the same as the Parayars did. The Parayars would take care of the lands and the Naickers would sit in their homes and enjoy the harvest. "Why has God made them like that, but made us like this, the lower-caste women would wonder, and wail aloud". (VV 7)

Within the Dalit community, the growth of the one sub-caste among the other cannot be tolerated and it brings the discrimination within the community. Education has refined the Parayars and changed their lifestyle by making them more civilised and cultured. The Parayar never depend on anyone they do many kinds of jobs as tailors, lawyers, masons, plumbers, drivers, conductors, teachers, policeman, and many other trade and professions. Before ten years the Parayars would get the Odaiyar offering from the landlord houses such as rooster or one or two pumpkin, sugar and rice. As more and more of the Parayar boys left the village for the education they stopped getting the offerings from the landlords. "Very soon after the Parayars had given up the practice of making harvest offerings to their landlords, the Pallars also stopped doing it. The landlords were angry with the Parayars for behaving like this and for spoiling the Pallars also". (VV 7)

The lands of the Caste Hindu was taken care by the Pallars and Parayars in order to bring rift and spoil the harmony between them the Naikers would ignite the vengeance in the hearts of the Dalit labourer who come to toil their fields. By doing so the Caste Hindus would bask in the warmth of the vengeance between the sub-castes to achieve the position in the politics. Saminathan's uncle Mariaraasu was tall and well-built fellow he was the one who watered Ranga Naicker's fields. The water from the irrigation channel has to be diverted to the various fields the landowners slept comfortably in their houses and it was the Pallars and Parayars who had to be outdoor in misty weather to water the fields at early dawn there was no one to care for them. Right to Ranga Naickers field was the one belonging to Palanivelu Naicker. The field was being watered by a Pallar named Karuppuswamy. "There were constant quarrels between Marraasu and Karuppuswamy about the irrigation water. Whereas Ranga Naicker and Palanivelu Naicker lived in peace, here the Pallars and the Parayars who were in charge of watering the respective field turned into sworn enemies". (VV-8) Ranga Naicker would instigate Marraasu and Palani Naicker would stir up Karuppuswamy. Without quarreling not even a day would go between them. Palani Naicker went a step forward and told Karuppuswamy to be aggressive and promised to take care of everything.

That day it was the turn of Ranga Naickers field to get water. Marraasu reached the place but Karuppuswamy had gone to divert the water to Palanivelu's field. Marraasu noticed this and he dug a ditch to divert the water to Ranga Naicker's fields. Karuppuswamy notices that suddenly the water got stopped. The quarrel broke up between them. Pichamurthy who had been working in the adjoining field heard the commotion and rushed there and said:

> Why did you divert the water out of the turn? Isn't that the reason for this unnecessary argument? Why all this fighting amongst us? Whether the fields are dry or watered, what is the gain to you? It's someone else who's going to reap the benefit, but it's you two who are fighting! Let it go, both of you. Don't come and shout like this in the fields in the middle of the night. The very sound of it is unnerving. (VV 9)

Karuppuswamy lifted the spade he was holding and he struck Marraasu hard blow on his head and he placed a stout stick on Marraasus throat and pressed it hard by his foot. Later Karuppuswamy came to his senses and knew that Marraasu was dead. Palanivelu Naiker paid off the police and managed to convince Pichamurthy about it. "After all, when one has wealth, one can do anything, cover it up, and get away with it"! (VV 11)

Saminathan was distressed and he felt that "Because we have no money, no education, they killed and buried my Chithappa in a ditch… as if it was all in a day's work, as if he were a mere dog or something. And yet Chithappa was such a strong man. If only Chithappa had not been drunk that night, that other fellow would not have been able to stand up to even one blow". (VV 11) He felt insane by the murder of his Chithappa and he felt that if the person of our clan found out the murder then he would have supported us but he belonged to Pallar so he kept quiet for this injustice. "We should get ourselves education, qualify as lawyers, and come back to put an end to this sort of injustice. It's only with education that we can get a proper understanding of such matter". (VV 12) He could not take up the murder of his uncle and he used to talk about this to his mother and she would say that it was your uncle's fate to die in the hands of Pallar. He got angry and said to his mother that "When the fields are not even their own? I'm asking you, why they had to fight and die for the sake of the landlord's field". (VV 12) She further said to her son that it was the coaching of the landlords that the Pallars are behaving so crazy. He asks his mother about the coaching she says that:

> They're the ones who are plotting to make sure our two castes never unite. This has been going on for ten or twenty years now. In fact even in your forefathers' time, there had been this enmity.

> I don't know how many lifetimes it will take for our two castes to come together as friends. The way the things are going, it looks like it can never happen. (VV 12)

Abraham continued

I've been observing this ever since I was old enough to understand things. Our panchayat president is a Naicker; the milk society president... Naicker; the cooperative society president... again a Naicker. Our fellows blindly vote for them and get them elected, and then go and stand before them with folded hands and slave for them. That's all the sense our fellows have!. (VV 14)

Saminathan noted that recently our people stood in the election and won the post. For which Abraham said that those victories are the slap on their face. Five years ago Pallar and Parayars came to an agreement and the Parayars stood for Milk society and the Pallars stood for co-operative society and all the votes were given to them and they both won the election:

> The Naickers became utterly scared. If the two castes were to work together and put up a common candidate, they could snatch away even the panchayat president post! They thought, all these years these people have been coming and standing before us with folded hands, ready to serve us; we mustn't get to a situation where we have to bow before them. And so the Naickers made a plan to destroy the unity between Pallars and Parayars. (VV 15)

Even now who has killed your uncle Marraasu it was a Pallar and how did Pallar do it was from the courage given by Palani Naicker. The Naickers tell the Pallars that "look, you and we are Hindus, and we Hindus must stick together". (VV 15) Before the incident happened Pallars and Parayars were together and if it was New Year or Christmas the Pallars would come to the Parayar street and enjoy and if it was Pongal the Parayars would go to the Pallar street and celebrate it and they used to address one another as 'machaan' and 'maaple'. Everything was fine until the time of Pongal festival when the game Kabadi was being held and the umpire sent the Pallar team out stating that they never followed the rules and a big physical fight took place between the Pallars and Parayars. In the New Year kabadi and volleyball games were held and both the caste people took part in it. In the finals, the Kandampatti Parayars won the volleyball match and the Kandampatti Pallar won the kabadi match. They didn't bother about caste too much but it was only after the death of Marraasu it was so much hatred built up between the two castes.

Many villages from nearby would come and join in the matches. Though there were so much fight within them but they would get along with each other as soon as possible and they had never gone to the extent of committing murder. It was once when the Parayar fellows won the volleyball trophy and when they were walking in the street of Naickers the Naickers asked them which place they were from the boys didn't answer their question. Ashokan asked the boys that if you all belong to our village which street are you from? Then one boy named Xavier replied to them as a slap on their face as "The Parayar street…also known as R. C. Street". (VV 18) Then the Naickers exclaimed about the Parayars behaviour and how arrogantly they replied and one of the Naicker told that the Parayar who replied was Muniyappans son who worked in Gopalasamy's house. This was the same fellow who came with his father who held out his hands for food but now just because he has got a bit of education he is behaving as if he is very important fellow. For which came a reply from the boys that "What's there so special about you people? If you're here, we shouldn't laugh, is it? We shouldn't talk? This is a free country. We will talk anywhere we like. We will laugh. We will play. And we will win. See, we have won this volleyball cup. Take a good look at it". (VV 18) Though the Naickers were furious, there was nothing they could do. And they muttered:

> At one time they were starving without even gruel, and now look at their power! And their clothes! Even better than what our children wear. When they're at the bus stand, we can't even tell who they are. Also, both the men and the women of their caste are getting educated. All this is coming from their religion. We can't let these fellows go on like this. The Pallars are better; at least they're still respectable towards us. (VV 18-19)

In the west of the village is a lake it is Seenivasan Naicker's well located at that place and many people from the street would go to take bath from that lake. The boys, elders and the women of their street would take bath in those well but Seenivasan Naicker didn't like that but even though he didn't say it directly to them but he told it to his worker Pallakudi Pachamalai who waters their field not to allow people to bath so he would chase the people coming to bath in the well. But the youngsters refused to go away they took bath as usual and Pachamalai went and told about it to Naicker. Then Naicker shouted at them and asked them do you think this is your father's well for which Joseph one among the boys said "Yes this well was dug by my father. So this is where we will bathe. All the wells in your farm and fields were dug by our people only. So we will go and bath in any of them. Yes! As soon as he finished speaking they all shouted in chorus, 'Yes…this is our well. We will bathe only here". (VV 30) Seenivasan Naicker was absolutely boiling in fury. He told to put thorny bushes near the well even after that the boys cleared the thorny bushes and they bathed in it.

The impact of education changed the minds of the Parayars and On April 14th they unveiled the statue and the people of the Parayar streets were in happiness. The speech was given by Naattamai and then Anthony gave a speech about education and he put forth Ambedkar's words as "Educate! Organise! Agitate!" this was his words and he spoke the importance of education for all and he addressed the people to follow the steps of Ambedkar. As the time went the Pallars were not happy with the installation of Ambedkar statue instead they made quarrels about the donation and they felt to have a statue for Immanuel. The Naickers started instigating the Pallars and asked them to come on their own instead of thinking of the Parayars.

Lokanathan Naicker asked Perumal about the troupe and the way they celebrated the festival for which the Pallar Perumal said he couldn't sleep that night as the people made a hell of noise by dancing, singing etc. when the Naicker asked him to protest against them. Perumal said "Aiyayyo! Don't say that, sir. From their street, many of them have studied and become teachers, lawyers, doctors and college lecturers... That's why they're not coming to us anymore for manual job". (VV 62) Chinnamma who worked in the Naickers field came to know about how the Pallars dance to the tune of the Naickers and said that "If a village is split into two, only the mischief-makers will celebrate".

The people who belonged to Pallar Street were fumigating the issue of police coming and asking them a question and the village meeting was held by the Pallars and one man spoke that they are Cheri people who are giving complaint against us. He stated that the Parayars are inferior to us and we are not untouchables or Dalits. We must get together with our caste people and make sure that the Parayars don't raise their head. The youngster of the Pallars planned to get the donation amount thousand rupees given to them and they planned to get their own flag pole and they made a flag pole next to the Ambedkar statue and they want it to be little higher than the Ambedkar statue. When they started to anchor the pole to the four sides of the Ambedkar statue the people of the Parayars told them to tie the thread little further from the statue or it will lead to unnecessary problems but the Pallars were stubborn and they spoke harshly. Next day Sesurathnam went secretly and cut the thread and he came and told to the people what he did. The Pallars were in fury to finish him off they ordered the village women to pack up and leave the house and the old men were asked to be in the chavady. The Pallars planned to make the attack in the morning as the men in the street would be out for wages and it would be a convenient time to finish them off. Sesurathnam was standing near the tea stall. The Pallar men attacked him Kalimuthu raised his arrival to aim at his head but his arms were cut and they chased him to death and he ran for life and he got into a house. But the Pallars went into the house and hacked him to death.

Once the Pallars and Parayars came and settled in the village, the village higher officials (*nattamai*) of both the castes planned to meet and sort out the issue:

> In those days the Pallars and Parayars used to be united… No accusation or anything. They used to address our people as "mama" and "machaan", and we also used to talk to them that's the way…fooling around…having a good time. Look what's happening today…Like snakes and mongooses we are! So much hatred, jealousy, bitterness…all this is happening only in our

> village. Even if there are any quarrels we should settle them peacefully. (VV 121)

Both the caste people gathered and talked to them and the compromise took place like Parayars should not to show the witness of the murders to the police for which the Parayars accepted and the mutual compromise brought the unity among the Dalits. And the village people spoke that:

> Let them say whatever they want to. We should not retrace our steps. What is past is past. But the children who are yet to be born must be able to live in this village. So let's trust one another and try to get along together. We must be our guard in case anyone tries to provoke us and create enmity between our two castes. (VV 130)

This was the constant message from the elders of both streets. Later on after the amicable situation of both the castes the upper caste people mocked at them "what sort of fellows are these? After so much killing…So much wandering around like refugees…they're supposed to be united again. Shameless fellows!" (VV 133)

Later on, both the Pallars and the Parayars mutually and collectively decided to nominate a person of their own caste to contest in panchayat election against the Naickers. Kaalaiyan was the first Dalit to win the Panchayat president election in Kandampatti. Then the people of the both castes said that "it's not enough that we have won in this Panchayat election. The Dalit voice must resonate in the state legislatures and in the national parliament…As Ambedkar, the champion of the downtrodden said, we must capture the levers of government power. Let this be the first step towards goal". (VV 134) From then on the Parayars and Pallars remained determined that whatever anyone might say they would never fight again and further lived together in mutual tolerance and friendship.

3.6 P. Sivakami's The Taming of Women

The Taming of Women (2012) written by P. Sivakami, is the Tamil Dalit writer it was originally written in Tamil as *Anandhayi* and it was later translated into English by Pritham K. Chakravarthy.

Raji Narasimhan (2012) states that two crucial junctures in the novel: one is the exchange between Anandhayi and her husband's mistress, Lakshmi, on the emotive, culture-specific issue of the equations between wife and mistress. And the second is the scene of Anandhayi lying on the porch of her home, stricken by gastric ailments, assailed by memories of the licensed sexual assaults upon her by her husband. These assaults constitute the stuff of her growth from adolescence to womanhood. The novel portrays the discrimination between men and women in a small village. This is the story of hard-working Anandhayi, married to a womaniser, Periyannan, and their marital travails. There is a struggle for power not only amidst genders, but generations and families within the village as well. In this novel, Sivakami portrays the struggle of the Dalit women and her sufferings by tracing the double discrimination within the men from their own community and from the upper caste men. Anandhayi who is the wife of Periyannan is ready to give birth to a baby but she finds her husband sleeping with another woman upstairs. Anandhayi hid in the gap between the steps and the wall after a long wait she heard the door open upstairs and hushed voices. A tall figure came down the stairs and stepped on the last rung when Anandhayi grabbed the hair bun tightly. That was it. Periyannan climbed down and released the woman from Anandhayi's grip and pushed her aside. Anandhayi crashed to the ground with a loud sob. Crone the mother of Periyannan helped her to get up and scolded him for his merciless act. The hussy women tied her hair carefully and adjusted her sari and crossed the compound. Anandhayi slowly raised with the crone's help. The water had broken. Dalit women face so much suffering in terms of mind and body they are not treated with respect and dignity in their own community. Dalit Men try to have contact with many women among their community and they don't bother about their wife and if a wife tries to question for her rights she is beaten and put under constant physical violence.

A new town rose up next to the sugar mill where there were electricity substation, plenty of rice mills, fertiliser godowns, granaries, all sanctioned by the taluk office, though that office was in another town. Dahandapani introduced new women who were Lakshmi to Periyannan. He fell for her beauty, which made him stay most of the days with her. Kangani an upper caste man had got an upper hand because Periyannan was preoccupied with Lakshmi hunting and had ignored both his contract and the political party. Poor Periyannan was going through a bad patch of luck and could find no new contracts. His fields were lying fallow and the creditors were knocking on his door.

Dalit men with the community treat women as slaves and they are forced to live with them whenever there is a need of Physical satisfaction. Even though Lakshmi is not happy with Periyannan she pretends to make things appear smooth. Lakshmi pretends to spend happily and at late night she elopes with Manickam. Periyannan was more irritated with her eloping and through MLA he gets to know that they were in Kodaikanal and gets her back. Periyannan wants Lakshmi to be with him always as he feels that she completes his life but Lakshmi wants freedom from this man which she never attains till her death. Lakshmi wanted to leave him but he wouldn't let her go. She waited for her time and took poison and she died. Periyannan burst into tears. Anandhayi as a wife also faced both physical and psychological violence with Periyannan. All through the life, she lived with the thought of her husband enjoying sex with other women. Gender-based discrimination is evident in the novel.

Within the caste, the problem broke out by doing so the Upper caste men make use of the situation to make the Dalit being put in prison so as to enjoy the power and dominance in the village. Iyyakannu's son Maharaja was grown now that he could reweave the thatched roof of his house all by himself and began to go water the fields Noollaikannu had grabbed an acre of the waste ground next to Iyyakannu's fields so he would water both, leave his hoe there and walk towards the pond Maharaja was always eager to return home once the sun went down so one day he opened the channel into his field and went to pick his underwear that was drying on the fence. Noolaikannun ran up to open the channel to his field, only to find the water half empty. He saw that the soil in Maharaja's field was soaking wet. Hey, you chap…' he yelled. 'Stop there, I say! Take a step further and I shall break your ribs'. He approached maharaja with his spade. Maharaja reported the incident to his father at once Iyyakannu leaped to his feet. Angamma controlled him to stay quiet and she stopped him. Kangani took up the things in his hand and he made her get an arrest.

All through the novel, the author reveals the dominance of the men over the women the subjugation in terms of gender is very evident and the men want to show their pride in having a relationship with many women. The Dalit women undergo so much oppression from upper caste men and from the men of their own caste. As the present chapter deals with the aspects of caste discrimination and alienation, the proposition of chapter – 4 entitled "Writing Dalit Gender" is to deal with the gender based discrimination. It also deals with how the issues of caste discrimination and gender violence go hand in hand is representing the Dalit self in the select novels.

Chapter - 4

Writing Dalit Gender

Chapter 4 deals with the evolution and the major happenings that evolved around the gender studies in the West further which influenced for the evolution of feminism in India. The chapter also argues that how Elaine Showalter's three phases of women's writing succinctly made a bold attempt against the male-dominated society and the need for accepting the woman rights are equal on far with that of civil rights. The chapter also focuses how feminism in India excluded the innate emotions and feelings of the Dalit woman hence the emergence of Dalit feminism is unavoidable. The chapter also deals with how the select Dalit novels argue for legitimate space in the male-dominated societies.

4.1 Introduction to Feminism

In the thesis "*Writing the Self: A Thematic Study of Select Dalit Autobiographies*" Siva Nagaiah Bolleddu (2015) mentions the terms "Sex", "Gender" and "Feminism" need to be qualified to understand them in the present context. Sex refers to the biological aspect; gender indicates the culture of the sociological and political dominance of men over women; feminism, as a theory questions the gender dominance based on sex. The subordination of women had been fundamentally justified on the grounds of the biological differences between men and women. The subordination of women needs to be theorised for it helps in challenging, subverting and expanding not only other (male) theories but its own positions and agenda.

Like many of the existing philosophical, literary and theoretical movements feminism is also Western initiated and Indian migrated school of studies. Feminists examine the experiences of women for all races, culture, and classes like American, ancient American, American Indian, lesbian, handicapped, elderly and the third world subjects. It aims at freeing the women from the oppressive restraints.

Bell Hooks (1984) in her book "*Feminist Theory from Margin to Center*" states Feminist and Feminism started to get into the stream as the people saw feminism as the war between the sexes than the political struggle to end a sexist oppression. The reasons behind the war between the sexes are due to the sexual discrimination, exploitation, and oppression. Feminism can end the war between the sexes as it can transform the relationships so that the alienation, compensation, and de-humanisation that characterise human interaction can be replaced with a feeling of intimacy, mutuality, and camaraderie. Eradicating the sexist oppression will bring equality in the society as it is the basic of all other oppressions. Racism and class oppression is also stemming from the sexist oppression. Sexist oppression is of primary importance not because it is the only oppression but it is the practice of domination that most people experience the male play a role of discriminator or discriminated against, exploiter or exploited. Though the sexist oppression cannot eradicate or eliminate all other forms of oppression it can make the other oppression intact as all the oppressions are connected to the social structure.

Feminism is the one radical political movement that focuses on transforming family relationships. Bell Hooks (1984) further adds that feminism as a movement ends the sexist oppression to bring a social change that will strengthen and sustain the family life in the entire household. Bell Hooks (1984) conclude in her essay on *Feminist theory from Margin to Center* as the fight against sexist oppression is of grave political significance- it is not of women only. The feminist movement is vital both in its power to liberate us from the terrible bonds of sexist oppression and it's potential to radicalise and renew other liberation struggles.

The term masculine and feminine are used only in legal papers and forms but in reality, they are like the two electrical poles.

Simon de Beauvoir (1949) states about the view of society to see man as he is right in being a man and it is a woman who is in the wrong. Women are always seen in terms of the body as women have ovaries and uterus and these things imprison her in her subjectivity. Women are often termed that she thinks with her glands. Men ignore the fact that they also have anatomy as they include testicles and they secrete hormones. Women are always seen as an object of sex as anatomy is women's destiny. The identification of a woman is determined by her biology. Betty Friedan says that women have to shed her immaturity that has been called feminity in order to get the full human identity. This crisis of identity was there hundred years ago and in order to overcome the identity the women have to suffer to become fully human.

4.2 First Wave Feminism

European feminism is initiated by Mary Wollstonecraft. In her book, '*A vindication of the rights of women*' (1792) argues against the augment that women are weaker or inferior to men. In USA Margret Fuller in her '*Women in the nineteenth century*' (1845) deals with women emancipation, education, employment, and political rights. Further Fuller had to study of similarity between "*Women are Afro-American prisoners*" Hence she paved the way for new consciousness among the Blacks and women. Literary evolution of feminism starts with Virginia Woolf's "A *Room of one's own*" (1929) and "*Three Guineas*" (1938). Woolf's argument rests on the reading a test in the light of gender-conscious. The grammar, structure, style, theme and images what role the writer gives for women identity.

4.3 Second Wave Feminism

After Woolf and the writings after 1960's, we call them as the second wave feminism. It is a sort of radical approach for women's rights. Simon De Beauvoir in her "*The Second Sex*" (1949) published in French argues that men wontedly mystify women. She also argues that women are oriented for the acceptance of male dominance. Further, she opposed the patriarchal oppression. She says "one is not born a woman but becomes one. Betty Friedan in her "*The Feminine Mystique*" (1963) demystified the male oriented oppression and called for equal rights and an end to sex discrimination. Further Kate Millett's

"*Sexual Politics*" (1970) is the first widely read work of feminist literary criticism. Millet focuses on the dual importance of representative women through the biological and cultural lenses. She studies the literature so far available as a record of male domination. She argues against (i) Capitalism, (ii) Male Power, (iii) Crude Sexuality (iv) Violence against women.

4.4 Third Wave Feminism

The Third Wave is considered as the timeframe from 1990's to present day. In fact it is influenced by postcolonialism and postmodernism. This wave tries to erase the boundaries of gender. Controversy and disagreement around identity politics between feminists in the third wave have escalated.

4.5 Elaine Showalter's Three Phases of Feminism

Feminine phase (1840-1880) women writers imitate male writer in form and style. The second phase is a Feminist phase (1880-1920) women writings for the women's rights. The third phase called the Female Phase (1920- present) uncovering the male mystifications on women rediscovering women's texts and women. Further Showalter's *Gynocriticism* (1979) deals with the emergence of women as writer and critics and it leads to female literary tradition.

Further changes in feminism are the Postcolonial feminism, Marxist feminism and Black feminism some of the text that represents the writings of the blacks are Alice Walker's "*The Glass Palace*", "*The Color Purple*", Tony Morrison's "*The Beloved*".

4.6 Feminism in India

Suriyakumari, A, (1993) states that Women are not only left out in the political sphere but also in the social, economic and historical spheres they are been excluded and hidden. When we trace the Indian history we find the poor peasants, Dalits, tribals, and nomads struggle but we fail to know the struggles of women in each and every phase of life. Suriyakumari (1993) brings out the survey of Altekar's shows how the women act as a weighing scale to know the strength of a family and society as a whole. According to him:

> One of the best way to understand the spirit of a civilisation and to appreciate its excellence and realise its limitations is to study the history of the position and status of the women in it... The marriage laws and customs enable us to realise whether men regarded women as market commodities or war prizes or whether they realised that the wife is to all her husband's valued partner whose cooperation was indispensable for happiness and success in family life.

Looking into the status of women in the Vedic period they were given due respect and value. The social evils like Purdha, Sati, dowry and female infanticide came into society when the invaders like Muslim, Mughals, Britishers abducted the Hindu women and violated them. Suriyakumari. A (1993) brings out the words of Shakuntala Rao states:

> The tenth and the eleventh centuries saw the advent and later, the firm establishment of Muhammadans in the country. When Hindu culture came into clash with a culture far different from its own, the leaders of the society began to frame rules and laws to safeguard their interest especially the position of women. Rigorous restrictions were planned on them...We find at this stage child marriage firmly enforced. The death of a widow was preferred to her falling into evil hands. Hence, self-molestation of a widow was enjoyed by the law codes giving the unfortunate victim the hope of heavenly bliss. Such and several other customs were introduced which curbed the freedom of women to a very large extent. This was done perhaps to save her from the foreigners and to preserve the purity of the race.

Suriyakumari (1993) says about the Hindu customs as absolute seclusion and restraint (of women) were not Hindu customs. They were unknown in India until Mohammedan times. No ancient nation held their women in higher honour than the Hindus... The reason behind female infanticide came into society when the parents of the daughter faced endless worry and misery. When the husband dies the remarriage is not allowed then she has to go with the option of sati and it was unbearable by her parents to see her burn alive on fire if she fails to be so then she has to face the consequence in the society.

So it leads to the undesirable fate of the female child to finish the life in the bud. Likewise, the women not owning property is also evident as the landed property could be owned only by one who had the power to defend against actual or potential rivals and enemies. Women were obviously unable to do this and so could hold no property. The women are considered to be strong in another sense as they give birth to sons who can contribute indirectly to the fighting strength to enhance the efficiency of the society.

Kancha Ilaiah's (2004) *God As a Political Philosopher, A Buddha's Challenge to Brahminism* deal with gender issues. He argues against Greek philosopher's Plato, Aristotle and Indian Philosopher's Vathsaya '*Kamasutra*' Kautilya's *Arthasasthra* and Manu's *Dharasasthe.* By the time Buddha began to discourse on his ideology and establish the sangha, Indian women were passing through dark times. The Indus Valley culture of equality has been reduced to oblivion, and its urban luxuries disappeared. After this, the Rig Vedic brahminical society was established in which women lost all their social and political rights. The Hindu religious texts and the Brahmins provided a theoretical framework for the enslavement of women. They used cha stity, prostitution, marriage and every other institutional arrangement was to reduce the position of the women in the society as a slave to the male-dominated society.

Ilaiah (2004) further states that in the beginning, the women were taking part in all the rituals along with the men they were allowed to recite the Vedic mantras and only during the time of Upa-Vedas and Upanishads their position deteriorated and from then on the family and society through their socio-political rights.

Ilaiah (2004) bring out the what these Vedas and other Brahminical texts put forth new rules for the women and stopped the women to think on her own and live a life of freedom. The wife should eat only after her husband has finished, and a wife who does not answer her husband back even under great provocation is praiseworthy.

Ilaiah (2004) traces the views of Manu as, a woman should in her childhood be under the control of her father, in her youth under the control of her husband, if her husband is dead she should be under the control of her son. All old women have to be under the control of their sons. Irrespective of age a woman was not supposed to act on her own will even in her house; she must always be guided by men. This, in other words, means that a husband is granted the right of possessing many wives but polyandry was strictly banned. He issued a moral dictum that a woman who was unfaithful to her husband would be born a jackel, would ferment with disease and so on.

Ilaiah (2004) traces the views of Kautilya who is the writer of *Arathasasthra* states that every married woman was to be kept strictly under control and constant surveillance. Kautilya sanctioned Kanyasulaka (bride price) which, of course, pushed commercial and trade relation into marriage system. He gave enormous powers to the state to punish the women. If a woman gambled, or drank liquor she would have to pay 12 panas. If a man and woman made signs to each other, the woman alone was to be fined 20 panas. If a woman held a conversation in a suspicious place, whipping might be substituted for fines. Like Manu, Kautilya also did not grant the social and political rights for the women.

Ilaiah (2004) gives the view of Vatsyayana, the Hindu view of women took a new turn, and according to him women were of two types, the ganikas who were provided pleasure to men in having learned the sixty-four arts of love making and the wives whose main duty was to produce male offspring. In this view, every nagarika (civilised man) had a right to have a harem of his own and the wives could be disciplined by every rigid rule. In Vatsyanana's view, women had no place in politics and state affairs.

4.7 Dalit Feminism

Sibhu Simon and Sarojini Sudha (2012) and Women, the most oppressed being in history, have begun to respond vigorously to subvert the conventional norms. The marginalised and subaltern women have found space to express their sufferings and experience faced for generations. The cruelty of the upper class, superior race, and the rich society are defined in their writings and it need not be considered as oppressive. The creative outpouring indicates the coming of age of women, especially of the subaltern women's literary tradition.

There is a testimonial of witnessing. The narrators are at the same time the victims of discrimination and also the witnesses who recount the trauma. Thus, the writings are both confrontational as well as subversive for they bring literature into direct encounter with the issue of caste, race, gender and religion.

The definition of feminism in Indian context is a complicated debate especially when we apply the feminism so as to understand the life of the Dalits, Minorities and Tribal women. Hence the emergence of Dalit feminism does unmask the mask of Indian feminism claiming that the Indian feminism is exclusivist and religious oriented. The Dalit feminism dares to interrogate the dominance of the Caste-Hindus of both men and women and challenging the imposed culture of silence over the Dalits for centuries together by voicing their feelings, the Dalit women pave the way for reclaiming their esteemed culture and represent themselves through their narratives. The Dalit narratives especially by the Dalit women truly aim at representing the innate and unexplored experiences of the Dalit women in the male-dominated Indian society.

Uma Chakravarti in her book *Gendering caste: Through a Feminist lens* draws the major women Bhakti saints of Maharashtra and Karnataka. Bakhtin's who belonged to this movement were drawn from the non-brahmins and the lower caste. It provided a democratic access to God and it opened up a new way for the downtrodden as well as women as they excluded themselves from the ritual order they were forced to live with.

There were two traditions within Maharashtrian Bhakti tradition they are Mahanubhav and Varkari. Mahanubhav form of Bhakti was famous among the untouchables and it admitted women and they outnumbered the men. The women felt the desire to escape from the caste-based brahminical social order allotted to them. Some misogynist women imposed doubts Chakradhar a preacher reputed to it by saying, Is there any difference between your soul and their soul? Why shouldn't these women come for the sake of religion? This radical potential brought an end to Chakradhar who was assassinated in 1274. Yadav kings Chancellor Hemadri's wife Demati deserted her husband to join the Mahanubhava movement.

Varkari tradition is a seasonal pilgrimage which attempted to blunt the radical critique of Brahminism through a modified devotionals within the boundaries of caste. This movement survived in Maharashtra having the main features of Bhakti and it drew saints from various locations like Eknath, Namdev, Tukaram, Chokhamela and many women saints also like Muktabai, Bahinabai, Soyrabai, Kanhopatra, and Janabai. These saints were from a low background like peasants, artisanal communities, cultivators, labourers, cobbler etc. Janabai was a prostitute she was sexually and economically exploited by her master but yet she had the religious understanding. Chokhamela is a cobbler and labourer his son Karmamela and his wife Soyrabai contributed much of their work to the religious movement. Bahinibai a Brahmin women saint was exploited by her husband but still in her poems she purifies his relationship and worships him as God. Kanhopatra is a lower caste prostitute in her poems she seeks the redemption of God. Ramdas a Brahmin saint resorted superiority even among the group of Brahmins within Bhakti movement and varna ashrama was there in Maharashtra even in an eighteenth and nineteenth century. Mirabai a princess of Rajput has written many famous hymns and broke traditional way of living a princess and became the disciple of Ravidas. Though her outrageous husband tried to bring her back to the kingdom, he failed so he put her in prison. Being from high caste she found her guru among the untouchables and remained with them and followed their ideologies and dedicated hymns for the untouchables.

A new way of the ideology of Bhakti tradition was followed by the saints of north Karnataka and was named as Virasaivite or Lingayat Movement. Most of the women were part of this movement and fought radically for the caste change in the society. They are Lingamma, Kalavve, Bonto Devi, Akka Mahadevi etc. This movement led to destroy the caste in Karnataka they were not able to change their state and so they become a group and practiced their own belief and tradition by marrying among themselves. Uma Charkaravathi (2006) states that we need to keep in mind that the Bhakti tradition gave the under privileged an arena to express their social aspirations, a transformed self-identity in a limited sphere but not a new social identity in the world of social relations.

Virashaivas are the followers of Siva and are also called as Lingayatas were the combination of egalitarian and spiritual excellence. It originated by Bavasa in the twelfth and thirteenth century being Brahmin by birth he opposed to tie the sacred thread. He later became the prime minister to King of Kalyan of Kalachuri and gave a shape to the movement. He encouraged the inter-caste marriage which was not acceptable by the Brahmins. A minister in the king Bijjala's court gave his daughter to the leather weaver it was against Virashaivas father Madhuvayya along with the bridegroom Haralayya were arrested, tied to the legs of elephant and dragged to death. Women made their presence so strong and they joined their husband to take part in the radical movement which brought a new vision of the men-women relationship.

Mahatma Jotibai Phule was the first man to establish an anti-caste movement for the liberation of the untouchables to put an end to the caste-based oppression, women subjugation, slavery, illiteracy, poverty, labour etc. He was born and brought up in Maharashtra and was well educated he married Savithribai he didn't have a child so he adopted a Brahmin child. He gave importance to education and he felt that only education can be the eye opener he termed the understanding of knowledge as Tritiya rate which means the third eye. He was inspired by Kabir and Tukaram and many of his friends were also the followers of the bhakthi movement he felt that Buddha will be the savior for the Dalits. He was not able to tolerate the Brahmins domination at every level of the society as they had their dominance in economic and administrative areas.

B.R. Mani (2005) states that in 1873 Phule founded the Satyashodhak Samaj. The weekly meeting was held in Pune it dealt with social reforms, the importance of education, the abolition of superstitious beliefs, using swadeshi goods, simple marriage, widow remarriage, fight against sati and opposing all the imposed brahminical tradition in the society was much in debate in the meetings. He and his wife Savitribai established a school especially for girls in the year 1848 and he set up 18 schools between the year 1848 to 1852 in various place some in Pune and some situated in the rural parts. Savitri bai was the first, in many ways, of the nineteenth century Maharashtrian feminist, taking up with enthusiasm the teaching of Dalit boys and girls in the schools...she thus remains one of the earliest role models of happily married feminist women. (p. 31) In 1860, Phule fought for the widow remarriage and he arranged a widow remarriage for a Brahmin widow and the baby whom she bore was adopted by Phule. He opened an orphanage and took care of many orphan children as well. He fought for the emancipation of the women as they did all the hard jobs in the field and they took care of the baby, household cooking etc. they were not like the Brahmin women though the Dalit women worked hard they were facing oppression within their community men as well the upper caste men. So Phule fought for the education for women the first women Tarabai Shinde wrote the book against the patriarchal order in 1882 and Pandita Ramabai a feminist and Sanskrit scholar founded Arya Mahila Samaj in 1882 to promote the women's cause.

A.K. Biswas (1997) traces about Sati or widow burning was a gory chapter of Hindu history since antiquity. It is a reminder of the dark age when genocide against the weaker sex was a creed, though not sanctioned by Shastra. This barbarous practice was a hallmark of Hindu culture and heritage. It generated vested interests in a section of the Hindus who even made a living out of the cruelty of women. It shows the worst fate of inhumanity towards the weakest link of the human society who has to gain respect, kind treatment and protection were consumed by the pyre. Sati was abolished by Lord William Bentick, the Governor- General of India under the East India Company. For Sati, there is no accurate statistics of the death of the helpless victims of the rituals. They were killed not by their enemies. Their lives were extinguished by those who sprang out of their own wombs: their sons. The women after the death of the husband were put into the funeral pyre along with the dead body of her husband. Every home did genocide of the women and it was the son doing it and he did not feel for the matricide.

S.M. Michel (2007) states that the women studies have appeared in many languages and the issues like abortion of the female fetus, the bride-burning, dowry, rape and domestic violence are represented and voiced out by the female writers. Mostly the Dalit women are affected and among the Dalits, there are people who are weaker. They are the Mangs (rope-makers), the Chamars (shoemakers), the Mochis (leather-workers), the Dhavars (tanners), the Lohar Ghisadis (iron-workers), the Kaikadis and Buruds (manufacturer of different types of baskets), the Telis (oil pressers), the Kumbhars (potters), the Tambolis (seller of pan leaves) these people are untouched by the urban culture, tradition, and education and suffer more than the Dalits.

The high caste people have a mindset about Dalits that they are dirty, lazy, quarrelsome, not reliable, that the women enjoy much more freedom than rural high-caste women and above all that they the women have no morals and therefore deserve to be raped. Dalit women work hard then the Dalit male as they work the whole day in the fields and additionally they do the household chores too but toiling in the fields the whole day they are paid very less when compared to the male folks. They sleep late and have to wake up early light the fire, cook the meal and walk a long distance to collect wood and water. Dalit women lack the freedom as soon as the man is in the house, the women is always under his control and has a subordinate position. She cannot invite her relatives when she so feels but has to welcome her husband's relative's cook for them and serve them whenever they come on a visit. She cannot keep her earnings for herself. Often the man takes the money she earns to buy country liquor and gets drunk.

Chavan (2007) a social activist puts forth the view of Dalit women as Dalit women work for the rich men and they become victims and people keep raping the women use them as concubines and finally they hush up everything by giving money and the Dalit women fail to voice out. The father and the son want to see the daughter and sister married and in order to send the girl out of the house they have to pay dowry. The more the money is given as dowry the girl settles in an expensive and wealthy place. The dowry also depends on the education and beauty of the girl. Once the girl is gone she is gone forever and nobody bothers about her and the bonding between the families is disconnected and if any problem arises she has to manage and be with the husband till she dies. As a Dalit women are not supposed to leave her husband but to stay with him, even if she suffers. When there are quarrels, she may only hope that everything will return to normal. She cannot leave his house and her children. For the sake of society, she is expected to put up with everything. Many wives are scared of being beaten by drunken husbands. And they still find no way to leave the man.

S.M. Michel (2007) further states about Dalit girls, who were not accepted as brides by the high castes and rejected by the men of their own caste, had no other possibility but to become prostitutes. Likewise, with the caste itself, there are various sub-castes and there are rifts, quarrels, inferiority and domination within them. Mahars who consider themselves superior to other Harijan communities of the area, will not at all tolerate mixed marriages with caste whom they consider lower in ranking, namely the Mangs, Doors and others. The castes have different cultures, languages, and behaviour. The Mahar are higher, the Mang or Dhor are lower, and we cannot give our daughters to them or accept their girls. If such a marriage took place, the couples could not live here; they would have to go away. Even conversion to another faith does not change this attitude. Caste is much more important than religious domination.

S.M. Michel (2007) further states that the Dalit woman face the worst discrimination as they won't have proper clothes, slippers to wear and they often think of the next day food for the children and family but the Dalit men are not worried about anything. The Dalit women find the difference between their situation and higher caste women's situation:

> In higher caste, the men bring home the money and not the women; women look after the household, but not outside affairs. We, Harijan women, are 'allowed' to earn money and our men have less tension because they can count on us. Somehow, we always manage to find some money and prepare something to eat. And if a woman works well, her husband relies on her more and more, and she has to work more and more. Often our men sleep quietly, and we cannot sleep because we think of our work and money. The men go to the bazaar, roam around and enjoy themselves. We always stay behind and work. We have no time like that.

Ravikumar (2009) states that according to Hindu dharma, Shudras and women are not supposed to perform the following six duties: (i) chanting the Vedas; (ii) practicing meditation; (iii) aspiring to renunciation; (iv) chanting mantras; (v) going on pilgrimage, and (vi) entering temples and worshipping gods. These laws create an opposition between the sacred and the profane, and they treat Shudras, dogs, cows and women as the four unclean objects. Women and Dalits are prevented from the pursuit of knowledge.

Sibhu Simon and Sarojini Sudha (2012) states that the Dalit women suffer from dual disadvantage; first, of being Dalit due to socio-economic and cultural marginalisation; and second, of being women suffering from gender-based inequalities and subordination.

4.8 Joseph Macwan's The Stepchild

The novel *The Stepchild* (2004) is about the community of weavers, the Vankars, is subject to oppression from the more powerful upper caste of the Patels. The rivalry between the caste itself starts when the Patels try to have a perverted feeling of the Sankara girl of the village Shilapur. When Teeho and Valji go for auction to Shilapur they come across the incident where an upper caste man threw a stone on the pot of charming young vankarvar women named Methi she was drenched and abashed and around her feet the broken pot was shattered. Methi uttered "Bastard, which mother produced an evil son? Mind your bloody language… you slut!" (SC 15) said the Patels and by saying so the men's eyes started to rove over the women's nipples visible through her wet blouse. This humiliated Teeho the protagonist of the novel who belonged to Vankavar community from a neighbouring village questions and fights for the atrocious deed of the Patels. The Patels were not feeling low for their behaviour instead they attacked Teeho and wanted to take revenge against him. Women are always been seen as sexual concubines for the male. It is more worst in the case of the Dalit women as they are considered to be as untouchable women in terms of caste and touchable in terms of sex.

Men always get into trouble and the suffers are always the women as the Patels, on the other hand, were agitated with the issue of Teeho attacking them and they wanted to take revenge on him so they were desperate to ruin Teeha's life. The love which Methi and Teeho had developed were known to these people and they were waiting for good time to spoil it "She goes around like a sati, let her be saddled with this one, it will straighten her up for life. If Teeha has to live this knowledge, his life will be miserable. There is no punishment worse than this" (SC 23). The evil intention of raping Methi underwent a change instead they planned to ruin her future. They called Methi's child marriage husband Chunthia and they told him that:

> We have heard that Heera is not arranging the aanu and somebody from another paragna are making plans to elope with your wife. The caste may be yours, but our village will earn a bad reputation! This kind of thing had never happened before in any caste. We have not let it happen. And even now we don't want it to happen. (SC 39)

For which Chunthia never agreed and said "You think I am a worm, don't you? Who asked you to take the responsibility of my aanu? I spit on your money…!' His words infuriated Meghi, his nephew Manji and his worthless son Nanio and Nanji said "Look at that! What arrogance for a bloody dhedh!". (SC 40)

The love between Teeho and Methi is so intense and they fall in love with each other at first sight though they belong to different paragna they go to the extent of marrying each other. At first Teeho fights and rescues Methi when upper caste men threw a stone at the pot she carried and from then on the vengeance between the caste starts and it leads to loss of many people. Though Teeho is not allowed to enter Shilapaar but instead of him his close friends Valji and Bahavankaka make a visit to Heera's house to fix the wedding it was at that time when Heera was in dilemma to give assurance for the wedding as there was enmity within the villages it was Methi who says to Bhavaankaka "There is very little traffic between our villages. I may not be able to send a message again; on the noon of the next full moon day, I shall be waiting for him, like Okha, here by the fallow land. Hire a van, if need be, and rescue me!". (SC 57)

Valji got the taxi to get Methi but Manji and Nanji took over the situation and they got Methi in the taxi and went straight to Keradia.

When Valji went to rescue her he was crushed to death. When Valji's wife Kanku asks Teeho to give acceptance to Methi's marriage he says

> Teeho has taken an oath bhabhi, if you have denied yourself the world in your widowhood, I have denied myself my desires in the separation from my friend. You've become a widow in a worldly sense, I have become a widower in another. Not Methi alone, but that very direction has become inimical to my existence. Bring that up again over my dead body. (SC 118)

Even after so many years Methi waited for Teeho's acceptance for marriage but upper caste men wrote a false letter to Methi as it was from Teeho, stating her not to wait and to go on to her in-law's house to Keradia. Even after so many years of the desperate life with Chunthia when Methi is about to commit suicide it was Teeho who rescues her and her child and gives shelter and safeguards them. Even at that point of time they never felt like starting a life together. As far as concerned the love between Teeho and Methi was not just physical it was more of pure eternal love. Kanku proved to be a best better half for Valji she supported him a lot. Valji understood his wife that she wasn't just his wife, but his true companion. Very practical, extremely affectionate and truly committed to his happiness. On the whole, she was more concerned about others, rather than herself. She mourned a lot for his death. It was Teeho who gave consoling words for Kanku "you need the grit to give up mourning, Bhabhi. The mother who weans the child away from her breast suffers more than the child itself; but for the child's own good she has to toughen herself. How long will you grieve?". (SC 106)

When a woman is deserted by her husband every man thinks that they can take over the women for their own. Though India is considered to be an independent nation but still the women are under the clutches of the male-dominated society. There came a time that Dano should take care of Kanku and her son as it was the last promise of Valji to Dano but earlier Kanku's sisters marriage was fixed with Teeho since Teeho refused to do so the next preference was Dano. While Dano proved to be a good companion, trustable cousin of Valji. It was after his death Dano took care of Kanku and Valji's son. Dano refused to

Marry Kanku's sister because the society will misinterpret the life of Kanku, Dano and her sister Monghi. When Jeevan asks about it, Dano asks him to be in his situation and requests Jeevan to marry Monghi "if my marrying solves your problem, then why just Monghi, for your sake, I would marry even a witch". (SC 126) Then they fix the marriage between Jeevan and Monghi and after their marriage, Teeho tells Dano to marry Kanku as it was a great shock to him at first he refuses and he starts to attack Teeho and when he sees Kanku he stops and asks Teeho to repeat whatever he has told him. Teeho was frozen but later he spoke "He was bent upon bringing Methi over. I reminded him of my oath and said that if you want me to marry, you should first marry Kankubhabhi. Only then will I marry". (SC 116) And later Kanku gave assurance of what Teeho said was true "You have not realised what he must have gone through before saying this much to you, Dana, and so you have sinned by hurting him. If you wish to safeguard your brother's dignity, marry me. Neither you, me nor Teehabhai has any alternative left". (SC 131) Even though they had many chances to get into physical they maintained decorum and they proved to be with high qualities and later on when Dano felt what Kanku told was right he accepted for the wedding and they got married.

Methi started her life with Chunthia after receiving the false letter of Teeho from the upper caste. But the marriage didn't work out well she had undergone many problems to make her life secure but right after the delivery of her first child her husband started treating her very badly and it went to extent that when Methi tried to safeguard her child from her husband she hit on him so badly and came to a state to finish off her life. It was at that time that Teeho rescued her and gave her shelter and later on due to her pestering Teeho accepted for marriage and he married Vali a cousin of Kanku.

4.9 Sharankumar Limbale's Hindu

With the deep thoughts in mind Miland, a Dalit was walking and a car stopped by his side it was Manikchand and Gopichand upper caste men they were twins. As the son-in-law, they lived in father-in-law's household. As Sitaphale didn't accompany them he asked Miland to be with them. Gopichand cajoled him saying can you enjoy lust after your youth is over? And Manikchand said that we did good deeds in our past life so now we want to sin. And Gopichand teased Miland by saying that "You must have sinned in your past life. That's why you were born a Mahar". (H 7) Manikchand forced him to get into the car and he said that as Sitaphale was not coming today, there won't be women either. But we will have fun drinking and dining. And Sadananad the watchman will arrange everything. It was always a usual thing for the upper caste men to enjoy with the women.

From childhood, Miland was brought up in dirt. And today he spins around with Gopichand and Manikchand in their car, uses their mobile and visits their home and he liked that change. He knew about their womanising. And even he took part in it and enjoyed the company of other women. He called his wife and his daughter picked the phone and he told her to convey to her mother that he won't be coming home tonight because he is with Gopichand and Manikchand. The car was on the road while he saw a woman with her husband on a bike and he said to them that he wanted to flirt with her. And he asked them no women today? For which Gopichand said we are fasting.

When a Dalit revolutionary Tatya Kamble was murdered by the upper caste Kavale family the village was agitated the Dalit women ran for shelter to the nearby fields. The upper caste men like Gopichand and Manikchand took over the situation by using the woman who was hiding in their fields. Miland heard the sound of women's anklet. Both of them were dragging her resisting body. They disrobed her she pleaded them to leave her. While Miland asked them to leave her because she was a Dalit woman and she came into the fields to save her life. And now you are killing her. For which they said she was a woman. And they were men and why do you seek caste even in sex? He pushed him out of the bedroom. He was angry he couldn't break doors like a hero and save her. Gopichand left Manikchand in the bedroom with her and came out. Later Gopichand went inside. Then it was Miland turns to get into the room after Gopichand, Miland went into the room he saw her she was a new bride. He gave her sari and asked her to go. Then he felt why he reserves, to tell the truth to the people was. If he was an activist he must have told the truth to people. He felt shameful for his deed. The last night incident still remained in his mind. His head ached like a wound filled with pus.

He thought of the young bride and he felt that would she go and tell others about the rape or will she remain quite. Then the whole atmosphere was changed due to the murder.

Ever since Sonali came to Achalpur, as a new bride, she was enchanted by the sound of dholaki drums. She was married to Prabhakar Kavale and she heard the drums and went upstairs to see the dance. Her heart ached thinking of the sweet and sour memories of her happy college days. She was given a dance recital at the annual function and that gained a lot of fame for her and the local papers published her photographs and interviews and along her side, in the paper, there were Rohit a Dalit boy son of Tatya Kamble she even praised him and it created anger with the savarnas. She and Rohit got to know each other only in the dance and they became close friends. While the savarnas boys sent the photograph of Rohit and Sonali dance together to her father. As soon as Baliram Patil saw it he felt angry. Sonali had the habit of writing poems and many got published too and when Sonalis dairy of poems got into her father's hand he mistook it and put an end to Sonali's education.

Sonali's restlessness increased daily she felt Tatya Kamble coming in the dreams' she thought of her future life and Rohit Kamble was always on her mind. Prabhakar Kavale murdered Tatya Kamble and Sonali his wife was witnessing it from the terrace after he got arrested one night she left the Bara and walked towards Bhimnagar. Lahu Mang saw Sonali and she asked him the way to Rohit home and he guided her. She reached Rohit's home and knocked the door. Rohit and his mother Savitha woke up and they were shocked to see Sonali and Rohit asked her the reason of her visit for which she told that she is going to commit suicide and before that she felt to meet him so she came to say about it to him. Rambhau came to that place with Lahu and asked Sonali to come home. She walked behind him. And now Sonali has entered into Rohit's heart forever by dynamiting a tunnel through it.

Rambhau asked Sonali the reason of her visit to Mahar. She said that she doesn't know and how she doesn't want to wait for the murderous husband so she went to Mahar. As soon as Rambhau heard the words he took the stick to beat her but his wife Kashibai stepped forward to save Sonali and even his mom Parvathibai stood in front of the stick and raised her voice stating that Prabhakar went to jail for killing a Mahar, enhancing the family tradition and now you kill your daughter-in-law and go to prison, enhancing the family prestige, even more, the irony in his mother's speech hit Rambhau Kavale. Rambhau and his father discussed Sonali and they felt to tell about her behaviour to her father as they have spent so much money on the wedding and the way she behaves is so mean. But they kept quiet because she might get angry and she will be a witness for Prabhakar. And if we throw her out of the house then Prabhakar will think that in his absence we didn't take care of her. Suppose if Prabhakar doesn't come out of the jail we will get her married to Sudhakar.

Miland was on his way to the hospital to see his wife Lakshmi for a second delivery. In the bus stop, he was attracted to women and he felt to have sex with her though his wife was not at home but when he went near her he came to know that it was Surekha and he knew her business and her husband was in jail so he ran away at full speed. Then he went to hospital and he came to know that Lakshmi was given birth to a girl child but he expected boy but it was a great disappointment to him and he thought of his debts then he met Gopichand and Manikchand and got money from him.

Sonali had her likings towards Rohit and she thought of committing suicide but the thought of Rohit made her happy and she gave up the idea, on the other hand, Rohit couldn't sleep in the night he came into the Bara and he shouted heavily as he couldn't enter into Sonali's house he knocked the door and screamed and he left to his home with tears. A grand pooja was performed in the temple. Dalit lady Draupadi reached the temple after sweeping the village streets. Vishnu Pujari had his eyes on her. She asked for Prasad and Vishnu Pujari told her to come inside the temple to get it she told that her place is near the steps how can a Mahar come into the temple. But still he asked her to get into the temple and when she entered into the temple he grabbed her she tried to release herself from his grip by shouting and later on Sudhakar entered the temple and she ran away and Vishnu Pujari face fell for the deed he has committed.

Vishnu Pujari after the incident he wanted to take revenge on Draupadi.

Meanwhile, a false complaint of sexual assault has been lodged against Narendra Patil by Surekha. Dipak Mane committed suicide in the prison when she came to know that his wife Surekha Mane has eloped with Mangesh Kamble. Sadashiv More and his sister Ranjana More went to the temple and he told to Vishnu Pujari that some evil eye has fallen on Ranjana and someone is performing Black art. Vishnu Pujari in order to take revenge on Draupadi he told Sadashiv that he has doubt on Draupadi as she doesn't come to the temple and she never gets Prasad to. And later in the afternoon, he collected some stones and he went on the roof and he cast the stones on some houses. Everyone in the village came out and Sadashiv More told people that it was Draupadi who did the black art and they went straight to her house she was stripped naked and she was taken around the village naked. The Draupadi in Mahabharata was not stripped naked. But Draupadi in independent India was naked because she was Dalit. The Bhimnagar people picked Draupathi up and went. The village watched all this like blind Dhritarashtra.

4.9 G. Kalyan Rao's Untouchable Spring

In the novel, *The Untouchable Spring* (2011) G. Kalyan Rao states about the sufferings of seven generations. The setting of the novel is in Andhra Pradesh about the Dalits who are there they are the Mala and Madigas. The elder karanam was extremely cruel he had no pity. He had a son and daughter; he gave his daughter to someone in Nellore region. The son-in-law had a number of *agraharams*. In the very second year of marriage, he passed away. Collecting the money she got by selling the land she returned home. She leased out the remaining land. The Brahmin from Kolla Dinna looked after the monetary dealings of the Karanam's daughter. He went to the extent of making Karanam's daughter pregnant. One day Kolla Dinni Brahmin died by vomiting blood and Karanam's daughter hanged herself, it was elder Karanam who killed Kolla Dinni Brahmin, his own daughter and the fetus in the womb. The younger Karanam did not feel for his sister's death instead he went and checked the money she left.

Elder Karanam took care of the fields with Subbireddi and Atchireddy. One day in the late evening elder Karanam went into the eastern part of the field. Only Atchireddy's mother Rangayi would sit under the banyan tree and wait for the elder Karanam to be killed. When Subbireddi and Rangayi came to sell their cattle in the market and get money for their living it was Karanam who saw Subbireddi and asked him to work with him from then on he worked under him and whatever money he gets he gives to elder Karanam to maintain the accounts. Rangayi felt that she should go to the native place so she asked Subbireddi to clear the account and take the money with him but when he went and asked to Karanam about the accounts he got angry and so far no one dared to ask him about the money and the accounts. Karanam sent Subbireddi and asked him to come some other day. The next day Subbireddi was found dead in the cattle shed as people reported it was due to snake-bite but Rangayi found that he was strangled in the neck to death as she found the dark lines in his neck but she could not say it out to anybody. From then she waited for elder Karanam to be killed. Mataiah killed Karanam as he was the reason to kill Narigadu. Each had different vengeance on the Karanam's Rangayi was the witness to it she refrained herself "The dark night hid within itself the reality of the lives of untouchable people and the lives of women hidden in the life of Yennela Dinni." (US 57)

Subhadra was married to yellanna. Pittodu brought up Yellanna in a different way when Sulochannamma saw her first she said: "She looks like the Karanam daughter and praised the girl's colour, hair, and dress." (US 69) Finally, Pittodu accepted for the marriage and they gave three rupees and six annas as bride price and got them married. The water would be first irrigated to the karanams and then to the reddys and then the potters, washerman and then finally to the malas and madigas. The water was irrigated but when the water reached Atchireddy's field he gave lame excuse that if the water is sent to mala and madiga then the pathway would be with water and the reddys cart cannot go on the roadway so he did not allow water for irrigation. That night Pittodu, Poladu, Musalaiah and Mallaiah planned to divert the water from Atchireddy's field and they made their plan success. Everyone in the village was surprised but Atchireddy caught hold of the four people and harmed them badly at that time Subhadra took the spade in her hand and went towards the field of Atchireddy and broke the canal and the water started gushing out and the people thought she was possessed by some goddess. People believed that it was a goddess in her because a normal untouchable girl would not be able to do such things.

Martin and Simon are the Dalits who converted to Christianity gave preaching in the town about Christ. They came to know that some land was barren they approached Karanam to ask for it but he told it was not barren land he refused to give but he approached the white man and told the situation and he took some people and sat in front of the white man's house and later he got the land and gave it to the poor farmers. The Christmas came they discussed to name the child and many people came and attacked Martin and they stabbed him and they attacked him and they left the place. Simon took Martin on his shoulder to save him but it was of no use. The upper caste people started to attack the mala and madiga. Many were killed, the huts were burning the smoke from the flame touched the sky. Sarasamma and Sasirekha turned to corpse then Simon took the child and he thought to save the child and that child is Reuben.

4.10 Kancha Ilaiah's Untouchable God

In *Untouchable God* (2013) Kancha Ilaiah traces the discrimination of the women in general. Men always considered them to be the superior and they considered the women to be of low birth and they were considered to be inferior. Several women were returning home after the long day's labour work. Harvesting the crops was mostly a female task.

> Men were men whatever caste they were born in; they tilled the land and fed the cattle but they would never cook, or weed crops. The division of the labour of men and women was so deep that it was almost a thing of nature; it was so old that no one could have said whether it was made by Gods or humans. (UG 1)

In the priest, Veda Shastri's house in the kitchen the women were wearing wet sari around their shivering bodies and cooking it gives satisfaction to Gods and they were preparing thirty-three different dishes. The young women cutting the vegetable in the kitchen felt that "All the hours of the day we skulk in this rat hole of a kitchen, cooking nasty food that we will never eat. We can only know how our food tastes from our men's praise or blame. I think Shudra women, Chandala women are better off than us." (UG- 12) Veda Sastry felt we must look for an alternative arrangement for producing children. He said that there was once a king called Nala who was born in women's womb as his father coupled with another male. He said

> If we could cultivate the habit of men mating with men, we could remove pollution from our lives forever. As it is we are constantly in peril from the filthy stink of women. They are liable to bleed at any time and destroy the sanctity of the sacrifice and the integrity of mediation; their wombs are poison cells. (UG 15-16)

Appa Rao had a doubt that why do women cook in wet clothes? Our Gods enjoyed the food cooked by men in times past. For which Veda Shastry smiles and says the same Nala who was born of a man was the finest cook in Aryavartha. He always cooked in wet clothes. Even Bhima was an excellent cook that's why Nala and Bhima are always praised first. The food was being served and people ate the food Veda Shastry said: "As we are inadequately manly we are forced to eat food prepared by spiritually polluted beings- women." (UG 18) The women in Veda Shastri's house were well trained. They were unobtrusive as ghosts, yet always alert for unexpected emergencies. They knew that if they committed a mistake in the home, they would be punished by the law of Dharma- just as Panchamas were punished for mistakes in the public sphere. Even in the upper caste houses, only the leftover food was eaten by the women. When Isaiah came to Dalit colony when they were having food only the men ate first when the women were asked to sit and dine "No, no, We women do not eat till all the men in the house have eaten" said Veeramma. (UG 194) When Isaiah says that in our case men and women sit together and eat but and he said that "Our women eats more than we men eat". (UG 195) Veeramma gives a reply to Isaiah that "No woman eats more than men. Men eat all the food and say we did not eat". (UG 196)

When Isaiah saw semi-naked women on the roads he asked about it to Jacob and he explained "There was a man called Manu many centuries ago, who wrote a book saying that lower-caste women should always offer themselves to the gaze of the uppercaste men. If they cover themselves, they will be assaulted and punished." (UG 183) The upper caste people treated the women and used them as concubine and sex workers they have to clean the temple and sleep with the priest. While saying this Elumalai's eyes became red "not from drinking liquor but from drinking history... the history of untouchable slavery...the history of women's untouchable bodies and touchable private parts." (UG 192) Their Gods were different their Gods too did the same thing with our women and also men. Their Indra God was known for raping and keeping our women. Jacob and Isaiah went to the bookshop to purchase some book he took the book on Rig Veda. He read some word in the book

> God has made the caste: the Brahmins from his head, the Kshatriyas from his shoulders and arms, the Baniyas from his belly and the Shudras from his feet. The untouchables and women weren't mentioned at all. He remembered the words of Genesis: 'So God created man in his own image. In the image of God created He he, Male and Female created He them. (UG-121)

The women of the upper caste and lower caste are treated as sexual dolls and concubines by men. They simply use them and throw away. Though the women who belong to lower caste are called untouchable but their body is touchable and they can be used as the men wish. Namboodri a Brahmin was twenty he went to Govinda Nair's house and he spoke to him and he proposed his wish for mating his daughter Sita Mahalaxmi. With this happy news, he went to tell to his wife but his wife was weeping and said:

> My hopes are crumbled. Do you really wish her to live in sambandham? With all the namelessness my life is better: she will have neither face nor name. She will be the mother of Brahmin children but shall remain an unwed Nair. Can her children become Brahmins, let alone Namboodris? Can they become priests in any temple? You foolish man, how could you agree? (UG 28)

She disagrees to give to Brahmins but Govindan Nair roared "A Brahmin-Namboodri- is a God of Gods on Earth. Whatever they ask, they ask only to increase our virtue. Our Gods said that, Whatever a

Brahmin asks, you must give it-whether it be wealth, cattle or daughter." (UG 29) Govindan Nair said that as a spiritual demand he will give his daughter only to Namboodris and no one can stop it. Sita overheard the conversation and started weeping. By spending time with her mother she has learned a lot about the world of women. But that world had no status of its own.

The day came where he and Sita were alone in the room and it was their first night. He tried to experiment all the nasty things of the sixty-four arts and it continued for many days and he said this is what Rama did to Sita and Vishnu did to Laxmi. She was forced to sleep with Namboodri. She begot three kids for him. Aryavartha was the only country where the Gods exalted the spiritual sex. He was reminded of the Rig Veda which contained slokas after slokas about how Indra, the God of Gods have loved women- not his wife of course- the apsaras, divine prostitute created by Gods to satisfy their own pleasure. He asked her how do you like this life, Sita? She replied "I live the life of a dog, shut in a kennel, whelping every so often. When my master caresses me, I fawn over him," (UG 39) Namboodri's sister-in-law Shiva Shakthi who was sitting on the verandah saw him coming she ran into the home like a rat that sees the snake glides into the rat hole. She was a permanent widow her head was shaven and she wore mundu and her breast was covered with white pallu. Her days went in doing labouring in the kitchen with wet clothes. Her relatives and other widows told her that she must not feel happy and free when she is alone but she really felt free in the absence of her dreadful brother-in-law. Namboodri's elder brother died two years ago he believed in sati, though it was not under practice he couldn't do anything. He felt that:

> She must surely have been looking at men coming and going on the road. Hah! If I die, she will fly into the world of sex and romance like a bird with ten wings. Don't I know how these women are inside, never mind their fasts and mumbling? And then my brother will cast down from heaven. No chaste wife ought to be alive after the death of her husband: it only means she's secretly waiting for life to give her a chance at debauchery. Why else live? Better to enter the fire and purify the soul. (UG 25)

When Isaiah comes to Benares he asks Jacob who is these women with white sari and their heads clean shaved Jacob says "They are widows, they come here to live. They have nowhere else to go. Their families sent them here." (UG 232) Only the upper caste widows were burnt on pyres because upper caste men feared they might pollute the family's bloodline. "Can women not become Brahmins? The scriptures regard them as Shudras, unclean. Bankim Chandra called widowhood a 'Vishbriksha' a tree of poison." (UG 238) Then he meets Mala she does research over there and she explains to him about the women she says that all the girls are a widow. Some of them look no older than ten. In spite of the law the people will marry off their girls very young sometimes too much older men, they become widows inevitably and then they are packed off on a pilgrimage to Varanasi or Kashi from which they are not indented to return. The lower caste women were treated as concubine they were made to clean the temple and they were forced to sleep with the temple priest. "No doubt that the men who control the ashrams feel like kings with enormous harems to boss around. They count their wealth in women's bodies. This is not as extreme or perverted as you might think: women have been an item of exchange for centuries." (UG 240)

Balaram and his wife Sakku Bai had a dream. It was the dream of educating their only daughter Saraswathi as they named her after the Hindu Goddess of Learning.

Balaram was a fruit vendor and his wife was doing daily wages. On the way, Balaram saw a priest sitting in the temple and teaching four children. He approached the priest and asked for his daughter's education and the priest asked him which caste he belonged to and when he said he was Shudra the priest said:

> I am a pundit and priest of this temple. Above all, I am a Brahmin. Do you think we teach Shudras, Chandalas, dogs and donkeys? Who let you march into the temple like this and ask me whether I would teach you low-born daughter a girl, a damned bitch puppy! Get out! Out of this temple! Take your defiling feet off my floor!. (UG 69)

Pir sahib asked Sakku the reason for the long face while cleaning the mosque and she explained what had happened. He asked her to send her daughter to Jahanara bee she has studied till the eighth standard and she can teach the basic letters. Saraswathi carried her books and along with it, a broom sticks so that people would think she is going for cleaning work. Mala tells to Isaiah how her Parents accepted to do her Ph.D. only when she told her parents that she would marry whomever they show as bridegroom but she should be allowed to do her Ph.D. she even explains the state of other women how even the present generation girls didn't even learn their letters. "Till recently it was believed that if a girl tempted the fates, such as by learning to read, she would cause her husband's death." (UG 238)

When Namboodri on the way in the bus he saw people wearing shirts and he felt that during his day's people were semi-naked. In this country where humidity and heat prevail it is good to see people half dressed and he felt that when he was a child in 1880's men and women wore the only mundu. Kerala women never wore blouses. Prophet Mohammed said to Arabs to come to Allah's mosque only with fully covered bodies wearing switched clothes from toe to head. Women wearing switched burkhas had come to spoil the women of Kerala. He felt how wearing clothes could be the end of all modesty.

Hussein and Saraswathi studied together in the school and love blossomed between them. Their parents accepted and nikah was arranged Saraswati name was changed to Mumtaj Bee and she went to her in-law's house. "A mosque education was followed by a mosque marriage and a mosque name. And a Hindu Saraswathi became a Muslim Mumtaj Bee." (UG 78) It was Friday and people gathered for the mosque but they saw Hussien's body in a pool of blood one eye socket empty and his private parts were cut and his chest was crushed and there was a note "ANY CUTORGAN DARES TO MARRY A HINDU GIRL THIS WILL BE THE FAIT" (UG 78). Balaram's house was so silent and outside the house hung a banner "IF MUMTAJ BEE DO NOT BECOME SARASWATI WITHIN WEEK SHE ALSO FOLLOW HER HUSBAND"[1] Under this someone has scribbled "*Any Shudra lens letter any were in the world will have a punishment like Sarwathi call Mumtaj Bee met.*". (UG 78) The news of the murder was spread in the newspaper. Many people gathered near the mosque to meet the chairman Yusuf Ali Khan. They discussed the murder and they asked to type a pamphlet about the incident and they asked the people to distribute it after the mosque and then they can take the sword and cut as many heads as possible but women should not be raped. The Muslim were planning to kill much more people. "HEAD FOR HEADS…TWO HEADS FOR ONE PRIVATE ORGAN." (UG 84)

4.11 Bama's Vanmam-vendetta

In *Vanmam Vendetta* (2004) Bama portrays the sub-caste struggles within a Caste and how the women in the caste undergo all the pain and sufferings are narrated. During a function within the village women are being put low as Jayaraju announced in the mike to be calm and then the programme came to an end and he asked the women to disperse and he told the men to wait for that the women started discussing that why are women asked to leave the place immediately and only men are allowed for public meetings and one women said "You seem to know about the law and everything…can't argue with you. Still…just because a woman studies a little, can she become better than a man? After all, a woman's woman and a man's man." (VV 66)

The rift between the Pillars and Parayar men brought many problems to the women of the community. After the murder of Parayar by Pallar the Pallar men made the women flee to different places and the Parayar men left the women behind and fled to different places. The police came and took the Parayar women under custody. The police haven't brought any women from Pallar street this made the women to wail and shout at the policemen. Many women have left their six-month-old child in the cradle and all the men have flown to a different place to escape from the clutches of the policemen. The women in the cell wept and made loud wail. "Who is going to come… What can they say…how can they get us released? No one's left in our streets. Do we have to rot here forever? asked Rosamma in tears." (VV 85) These women were innocent and they were not aware of the situation. Chellakili begged the police guard, 'Ayya, you've brought all of us here by playing a cruel trick on us and locked us up like this. We have just returned from our daily jobs, and everything has been left undone at home. What crime have we done that you have locked us up like this? We don't even know the detail of what happened in the village, ayya.' (VV 85) The inspector came the next day and released the old women and mother of the infants but chellakili and other sixteen women were locked up in the cell again. As they were being escorted back, one of the policemen kicked chellakili in the lower belly with his boots and said "so you complained to the circle inspector about us, eh? We'll rip up your mouth if you utter another word!" (VV-86) Another policeman hit her hard on her lower back with his lathi. Chellakilli curled up and collapsed on the floor of the cell. "As she lay there on the floor of that police lock-up, she felt a sharp pain in her belly... And ...she had an abortion right there. She had lost her baby. What agony Chellakili suffered..." (VV 86) After seven years she was carrying her baby but the policeman has kicked her and the baby. The women around Chellakili consoled her.

There were no men left in the Parayar Street only a few women were there and they were determined to take the corpse of their men and clear it. Rosemary drove the cart and brought the corpse. "The women gathered together, took the bodies in the cart to the graveyard, dug a big grave all by themselves, and buried all three bodies in that single grave". (VV 87) The policemen were astonished to see the women doing the burial themselves. "these she-donkeys has so many guts, eh, they remarked". (VV 87) The next day policemen went into the Parayar street and started beating the women with lathis chasing them as they ran and raining blows on them and cursing them in the foulest language. They entered every street and every house thrashing all the women by asking about their hidden husbands. Thirty or forty of the policemen went around entering every single house, dragging the women out into the street, and beating them up. With no regard even for the infants and aged. When the beating finally stopped the women, horribly swollen with bruises all over, sat and cried. "Even our husbands have never beaten us like this. Are these fellows' beasts from the jungle... are they drunk and mad... how can they hit us like this... see how the blood has clotted and turned black..." wailed Irudaya Mary loudly. (VV 89) The men of both Pallar and Parayar clang were dispersed to various places, some of them were in nearby villages, some were in the forest and some went in search of new jobs to distant places to safeguard themselves. While the women were left all alone in the streets and they managed by milking the cow and distributing to other women and they were leading their life with the little food they had and they never went out for any work. Even to go to market they have to cross the Pallar Street. The upper caste people were basking in this issue of the lower caste. Slowly the life returned to normal.

4.12 P. Sivakami's the Taming of Women

P. Sivakami (2012) in her novel *The Taming of Women* reveals the plight of women their hardships faced in a family through the main character Anandhayi it was her delivery time she paced up and down in the dark room. Her contractions had started by the dawn she knew that the baby would be born. She had been aware of it for the past week. After all, she had already given birth to four. Wouldn't she know? Muthakka unfailingly arrived, as she had been there for the previous deliveries too. Last week they had been skirmishes with her husband. Because a distant cousin had whispered secretly to her that "I saw machchan last week near the blacksmith, with a woman." (TW 1)

Anandhayi looked around for Muthakka. Her bed was empty and she felt a sharp spasm. She looked at the latch and it was undone. She pushed the door but it couldn't be open. "Witch. She's locked it from the outside and gone to sleep with her younger brother," Anandhayi grumbled. 'Let her get back, huh' and she didn't look away from the window and she said 'There she is….my dear hussy… oh no, that is not Muthakka. She is too tall. Now who is this new harlot? She has pinned jasmine in her hair bun. Her satin blouse shines like a glow-worm…there she is, going up the stairway… she's gone up!'. (TW 2) Anandhayi was conscious about the hussy women who went upstairs Muthakka ignored her and went to bring the dhobi women who help her in delivery. Anandhayi hid in the gap between the steps and the wall after a long wait she heard the door open upstairs and hushed voices. A tall figure came down the stairs and stepped on the last rung when Anandhayi grabbed the hair bun tightly. That was it. The crone her mother-in-law woke up and, picking up her stick, called out in a grainy voice, 'who's that?' Periyannan climbed down and released the woman from Anandhayi's grip and pushed her aside. Anandhayi crashed to the ground with a loud sob. Crone helped her to get up and scolded periyannan for his merciless act. The hussy women tied her hair carefully and adjusted her sari and crossed the compound. Anandhayi slowly raised with the crone's help. The water had broken. Forgetting her stringent cleanliness the crone rested Anandhayi against the wall and helped her in delivery.

Kala the elder daughter of Anandhayi always visits Mariayyi's house taking Arul with her. Arul was the fifth girl of Anandhayi. Mariayyi had a crazy brother, Dingumalli who speaks very chaste Tamil and his house was full of books this was the reason Kala would go there under the guise of entertaining the baby. Dingumalli gives her a book with the title 'pullivettaikku poonapullimaan' (that deer that went on a tiger hunt) the moment she took the book she left the baby in the cradle and sat to read the book. Periyannan enters the house with files and asks for Kala he finds out the book she was reading and pounces on Anandhayi by holding her hair.

Kala came of age Periyannan did not organise a big function for Kala. He decided to do something along with her wedding. There was a change in Kala's attitude which wasn't liked by Mani even her desire for learning cycle angered her father and ended up by beating Anandhayi. Dahandapani introduced new woman Lakshmi to Periyannan. He fell for her beauty, which made him stay most of the days with her. Mani fails in his exams and Lakshmi supports him to study further. One day Anbu the youngest kid of Periyannan tells his father that someone visited Lakshmi. This angers him which brings a quarrel between them. He hits her with that Lakshmi gets angry and takes a sickle and goes after him in order to help his father Mani kicks her on the chest, cursing 'do even call yourself women?' Periyannan took over it and storms heavily on her chest and stomach. Lakshmi was more concerned about Mani's reaction towards her since she felt him as her own brother. Lakshmi escaped to her parent's house Periyannan wastes all his money hunting for her. Finally, he gets her and brings her back promising that he will never raise his finger on her or to ever be suspicious. Finally there was peace and he thought everything was set in right but it wasn't. This time, she left no clue as to where she could have gone.

The kangani had got an upper hand because Periyannan was preoccupied with Lakshmi's hunting and had ignored both his contract and the political party. Poongavanam works in supervisor's house she was very fond of Neelaveni and called her akka casually during her conversation she found time to praise Lakshmi to veni. 'She is taller than you and much fairer.' And she also asks her why she doesn't talk to Manickam this question makes her to thinking about the incident which happens years back. When Manickam was in his adolescence, Veni too was much younger. One night there was a huge storm and there were visitors in the house. Kangani woke him up who was sleeping out on the thinnai and asked him to go inside and sleep. Veni offered her bed to him and she took a sheet and lay down. Just as Veni was dropping off to sleep, she felt a hand roam her thigh. She slapped it off. She sprang up and opened a window she saw a foam climb into the cot and lie down she couldn't believe what had just happened after that night Manickam and Veni never looked at each other again.

As the days pass by Anandhayi got aborted and for the next four days she lay in her bed, not stirring, and Lakshmi took care of her. Lakshmi started working alone in the fields sometimes Dhanam the second daughter of Anandhayi was in her tenth grade she was no longer interested in her studies. One day she disappeared at night around eight. Anandhayi went searching for her and found her in the coconut field. There in the darkness, she could see two people almost coupling. It was Dhanam and the preacher's son, Daniel. She warns her saying that she will complain to her father. After that day she brings Daniel to her home in the afternoon in everyone's absence. But Lakshmi caught them and sends Daniel to his home. Before she could complain to Anadhayi about the incident, Dhanam wails aloud. Not aware of the situation she scolds both but Anadhayi's guessed what had happened. From that moment Dhanam takes advantage of the things and starts irritating Lakshmi by tearing up her clothes, mixing cow dung in her bathwater.

When Kala arrives at his mother's home Anandhayi prepares chicken curry. When everyone sits to eat she observes her father piling the meat on to Lakshmi's plate. The very night Lakshmi pretends to spend happily and at late night she elopes with Manickam. Periyanna was more irritated with her elope and through MLA he gets to know that they were in Kodaikanal and bought her back Anadhayi gets addicts to tobacco.

Lakshmi wanted to leave him but he wouldn't let her go. She waited for her time and took poison and she died. Periyyanna burst into tears. Dhanam as usual skipping the school when Periyanna got a complaint against her. Mani caught them near the bus stand. He hit Daniel and caned her. Daniel committed suicide and Dhanam too thought of ending up her life but Anandhayi saved her and got her married to another person. Now Anandhayi became an old grandmother but still her condition was same enquiring about her husband but still she pretend not to bother about him.

The present chapter deals with the evolution of gender studies in India and how the exclusivist feminist ideologue of the elite oriented Indian feminism was questioned by the Indian Dalit writers. The chapter also deals with how the Dalit Gender Studies emerged as a unique form of literary representation that paved the way for the rights of the women of all the marginalised sections in India. The chapter also deals with how the select Dalit novels are instrumental in constructing the Dalit gender identity in India.

Chapter - 5

Conclusion

The main objective of the present study is to bring out the common issues in the select works. Instead of going for a mere textual analysis, the scholar did an in-depth thematic study. Being entitled, *"Narratives of Deconstruction: A Postcolonial Study of Select Dalit Novels"* the present study is with an aim of studying the life aspects of Dalit communities for which a select Dalit Novels are taken for research. The reason behind selecting Dalit novels among the other literary forms is that Dalit novels remain a successful genre in representing the issues of Dalit culture and movements in Dalit idiom. It is also through Dalit Novels the writers present their sufferings, sorrows and victimisation due to the oppressive culture of Hinduism. Through their memories and personal narratives, the Dalits reconstruct their broken and long silenced history and able to demonstrate about their rights and identity. They also use their fiction to reconstitute themselves with the rest of Dalit communities promoting their language, culture. Highly influenced by B.R. Ambedkar and his philosophy, the Dalit writers use their Novels as alternative literature to the literature produced by the elites. It is through their life narratives, Dalits talk about the significance of education and self-assertion that lead to self-respect and empowerment. Being thematic in nature, the thesis is in five chapters.

5.1 Summing Up

The introductory chapter entitled *"Dalit Literature: Views and Reviews"* deals with the literary meaning of Novels in general and in Indian context in particular. The emergence of Dalit literature as an alternative one to the mainstream literature and the success of Dalit Novels in representing the Dalit self in Dalit idiom is the core content of the chapter.

Chapter-II entitled *"Dalit Novel in English and in Translation"* deals with how the oppressive culture of the Hinduism did not allow the Dalits to pursue knowledge since the time of the Vedas and excluded them from knowledge centres and also how the Dalits who turned against the monopoly of the Brahmins are ill-treated and killed. This kind of exclusion from schools and colleges is challenged by Mahatma Phule and Ambedkar who educated the Dalit masses about the value of education. It also deals with how the writers faced severe punishments and exclusion in schools and colleges. It is studied that the Dalit writers considered education has potential for the liberation of the Dalits and enables them to challenge the hierarchical structure and the ideology in Indian education system.

Chapter-III entitled *"Writing the Caste Discrimination and Alienation"* deals with the form and nature of discrimination and how the Dalits are humiliated and exploited at work and in public places. It is also studied that the Dalits are forced to do labour for unpaid wages and kept away from all social provisions and privileges.

Chapter-IV entitled *"Writing Dalit Gender"* deals with the construction of Dalit Gender. The study explores the limitations and exclusions of Western feminism and feminism in India. As the Western feminism excluded the Black women and their writings, feminism in India excluded the Dalit women and their writings. In Indian context, the Dalit women are influenced by Dr. Ambedkar and they became his followers. Bama and P. Sivakami are the writers of such Dalit consciousness who clearly depicted that the problems of women in India and that of the Dalit women are quite different. As a remedy for these problems, the writers remained staunch followers of Ambedkar and illustrates how education and self-assertion redeem the Dalit women from the problems of caste and gender.

The Concluding chapter deals with the findings of the study and they are given in this note under the title Conclusions and Suggestions.

5.2 Conclusion and Suggestions

Having summed up the study, the following points are the conclusions and suggestions of the present research:

(a) Quest for identity is an important aspect of the Dalit Novels. The Dalit Novels in general are attempted to re-write the caste history of the Dalits.

(b) Dalit Novels demand for the legitimacy of the due space in history, culture, literature, economy and politics.

(c) Influenced by Ambedkar, the authors of the Dalit Novels deal with the aspect of asserting the Dalit self, which in turn is aimed at the liberation of the Dalits.

(d) The Dalit Novels are not merely the writings of vengeance to spread hatred against the caste Hindus but also to promote the heritage of the Dalits.

(e) The Dalit Novels are aimed at rebuilding society to promote honour, dignity, justice and equality.

(f) The subjectivity of the Dalit Novel needs to be understood in terms of the communal self.

(g) The very emergence of the Dalit Novels is a form of the Dalit resistance because Dalits are using this opportunity to assert their identities through their writings. The growing number of Dalit Novel is a clear instance of how Dalits have been breaking the traditional silence.

(h) Much research is to be done in Dalit Novels bringing the Novels in native languages into English.

(i) Sub-caste issues will also be given priority and the sub-grouped Dalits whose fictions are in oral languages need to be translated and research will be carried out on such works.

References

Primary Sources

Bama (2008). Vanmam-Vendetta. Oxford University Press, New Delhi.

Ilaiah, Kancha (2013). Untouchable God. Samya, Kolkata.

Limbale, Sharankumar (2010). Hindu. Samya, Kolkata.

Macwan, Joseph (2004). The Stepchild. Oxford University Press, New Delhi.

Kalyan Rao, G. (2010). Untouchable Spring. Orient Black Swan, Hyderabad.

Sivakami, P. (2012). The Taming of Women. Penguin Books, New Delhi.

Secondary Sources

Agarwal, Supriya (2011). Telling lives: Tales of Oppression, *Impressions,* Vol. 4, No. 2. pp. 1-4.

Ahmad, Imtiaz and Shashi, Upadhyay Bhushan (2010). Dalit Literature: A Perspective from Below, Dalit Assertion in Society, Literature and History. Orient Black Swan, Hyderabad, pp. 10-250.

Ambedkar, B. R. (2007). Annihilation of Caste. Critical Quest Publications, New Delhi, pp. 4-25.

Anand, S. (2003). Touchable Tales: Publishing and Reading Dalit Literature. Navayana, Pondicherry, pp. 3-10.

Anitha (2015). Aesthetic in Dalit literature, *International Journal of Multidisciplinary Research and Development*, Vol. 2, No. 8, pp. 210-211.

Azhagarasan and Ravikumar (2012). The Oxford India Anthology of Tamil Dalit Writing. Oxford University Press, New Delhi, pp. 1-298.

Basu, Tapan (2002). Translating Caste. Delhi University, New Delhi, pp. 1043.

Beauvoir, De Simone (1949). The Second Sex. Vintage books, New York. pp. 1-189.

Bhagavan Manu and Anne Feldhaus (2008). Claiming Power from Below. Oxford Press, New Delhi, pp. 14-30.

Bharathi Thummapudi (2008). A History of Telugu Dalit Literature. Kalpaz Publication, New Delhi, pp. 13-237.

Bhosale, B.V. (2014). Sociology of Dalit literature, ABD Publishers, New Delhi, pp. 1-94.

Biswas, A.K. (1997). Sati: Saga of a Gory Practice. Blumoon Books, New Delhi, pp. 1-57.

Bolleddu, Siva Nagaiah (2015). Writing the Self: A Thematic Study of Dalit Autobiographies. Kalpaz Publication, New Delhi, pp. 1-200.

Brizee, Allen and Tompkins (2010). Feminist Criticism from 1960-Present, Weebly.com, Online; Accessed on 19 September 2016, Also available at http://mrbarkersneighbor-hood.weebly.com/.

Burgess, Anthony (2016). Types of Novel, Encyclopedia Britannica, Online; Accessed on 9 June 2016, Also available at https://www.britannica.com/art/novel/Typesof- novel

Burk, Denny (2013). What is the Meaning of Sex, Crossway, Online; Accessed on 4 October 2015, Also available at http: www.wtsbooks.com/common/ pdf_links/97814335 36090.pdf

Chakravarti, Uma (2006). Gendering Caste: Through a Feminist Lens. Street, Kolkata, pp.1-100.

Chavan, Dilip (2011). Emergence of Dalit Literature in Translation: Towards a Critical Theory, Online Accessed on 4 September 2015, Also available at http://drdilipchavan. blogspot.in/.

Chinna Rao, Yagati (2008). Dalits Struggle for Identity. Hyderabad Book Trust, Hyderabad, pp. 10-30.

Chitkara, M. G. (2002). Dr. B. R. Ambedkar and Social Justice. A P H Publishing House, New Delhi, pp. 1-50.

Dangle, Arjun (1994). Poisoned Bread: Translations from Modern Marathi Dalit Literature. Orient Black Swan, Mumbai, pp. 1-325.

Dasan, M., V. Pratibha, Pradeepan and Chandrika (2011). The Oxford Anthology of Malayalam Dalit Writing. Oxford University Press, New Delhi, pp. 5-290.

Deepak, K.P. (2013). Dalit Literature after Independence, Literalism-The Republic of Letters, Online; Accessed on 9 June 2015, Also available at http://literarism.blogspot.in/2013/11/dalit-literature.html.

Fernandes, Walter (1996). The Emerging Dalit Identity: The Re-assertion of the Subalterns. Indian Social Institute, New Delhi, pp. 15-78.

Franco, Fernando (2002). Pain and Awakening: The Dynamics of Dalit Identity in Bihar, Gujarat and Uttar Pradesh. Indian Social Institute, New Delhi, pp. 14-42.

Freedman, Jane (2001). Concepts in the Social Sciences-Feminism. Open University Press, Buckingham, pp. 1-10.

Friedan, Betty (1963). Feminine Mystique. W.W. Norton, New York, pp. 1-239.

Gaijan, M.B. (2007). Dalit literature Tradition in Gujarat: A Critical Study. Gujarat Dalit Sahitya Akademi, Ahmedabad, pp. 1-100.

Geetha, K.A. (2012). A Dalit among Dalits- The Angst of Tamil Dalit Women, Cross/ Culture, Online; Accessed on 21 August 2016, Also available at https://www.questia.com/library/journal/1P3-2659445321/a-dalit-among-dalits-the-angst-of-tamil-dalit women

Guru, Gopal (2009). Humiliation: Claims and Context. Oxford University Press, New Delhi. pp. 1-50.

Herrera, Nancy Cooke de (1994). *Beyond Gurus: A Woman of Many Worlds*. Rupa, New Delhi, pp. 1-48.

Hill, Collins Patricia (2008). *Towards Black Feminist Thought*. Routledge Publication, New York, pp. 12-55.

Hooks, Bell (1984). Feminist Theory from Margin to Center. South End Press, United States, pp. 1-40.

Ilaiah, Kancha (1996). Why I am not a Hindu. Samya, Kolkata, pp. 5-45.

Ilaiah, Kancha (2004). God as Political Philosopher: Buddha's Challenge to Brahmanism, Samya, Kolkata, pp. 1- 35.

Irudayam, S. J., Aloysius, Jayshree P. Mangubhai and Joel G. Lee (2011). Dalit Women Speak Out. Zubaan Publications, New Delhi, pp. 1-55.

Jamdhade, Dipak Shivaji (2014). The Subaltern Writing in India: An Over view of Dalit Literature, *The Criterion An International Journal in English*, Vol. 5, No.3. pp. 86-89.

Jayakar, Joseph (2014). The Predicament of Dalit in Untouchable Spring, Online Accessed on 23 December 2016, Also Available at iosrjournals.org iosrjhss/papers/Vol19-issue3/ Version-1/G019314244.pdf.

Joshi, Poornima (2013). Review of Untouchable God, Online Accessed on 19 December 2016, Also Available at http:// kindlemag.in/review of untouchablegod/

Johnson, Lewis Jone (2016). Feminism Definition, About Education, Online; Accessed on 23 August 2016, Also available at http://womenshistory. about. comod/femin ism/ a/feminism.htm/.

Kaur, Tanveen (2014). The Formation of Categories of Hurt and Injury: A Reading of different constituencies in Sharan Kumar Limbale's Hindu, Online Accessed on 1 Feburuary 2017, Also Available at www.researchscholar.co.in downloads/5-tanveenkaur. pdf.

Kavitha, K. (2014). Dalit Literature in India, *Paripex: Indian Journal of Research*, Vol. 3, No. 4, pp. 239-240.

Kumar, Raj (2010). Dalit Personal Narratives: Reading Caste, Nation and Identity. Orient Blackswan, New Delhi, pp. 1-55.

Lakhadive, Rajkumar (2016). Recent Trends and Developments in Indi English Fiction, International Journal of Engineering Technology, Management and Applied Science *(IJETMAS),* Vol. 4, No. 3, pp. 111-116.

Limbale, Sharankumar (2004). Towards the Aesthetics of Dalit Literature: History, Controversies and Considerations. Orient Black Swan, Hyderabad, pp. 1-40.

Limbale, Sharankumar (2013). Dalit Literature and Dalit Writer-Generally about Books, Online; Accessed on 27 January 2015, Also available at http: www.generallyaboutb ooks.com/ 2013_05_01_archive.html/.

Limbale, Sharankumar (2015). Critical Summary of the Dalit Literature and Aesthetics, Critical Aesthetics, Online; Accessed on 31 March 2015, Also available at https:// criticalaesthetics2015.wordpress.com/2015/09/26/1-critical summary-of-the-dalitliterature- and-aesthetics-by-sharankumar-limbale/.

Louis, Prakash (2003). The Political Sociology of Dalit Assertion. Gyan, New Delhi, pp. 1- 41.

Mackinnon and Catherine (1991). Towards a Feminist Theory of a State. Harvard University Press, New York, pp. 1-55.

Malagatti, Aravind (2007). Government Brahmana. Orient Publications, New Delhi, pp. 1-110.

Mandavkar, Pavan (2015). Indian Dalit Literature Quest for Identity to Social Equality, *Giap Journals*, Vol. 3 No. 2, pp. 60-69.

Mani, B.R. (2005). De-Brahminising History: Dominance and Resistance in Indian Society. Manohar, New Delhi, pp. 1-35.

Manoja, G. (2014). The Beginning of the Marati Dalit Literature, *International Journal of English Language Literature and Humanitics*, Vol. 2, No. 8, pp. 1-5.

Michel, S.M. (2007). Dalits in Modern India Vision and Values. Sage publications, New Delhi, pp. 1-360.

Mishra Arti and Anjali Srivatsava (2016). Feminism in the Novels of Chetan Bhagat, *International Journal of English Language, literature and Humanities (IJELLH)*, Vol. 4, No. 2. p. 231.

Mishra, Jugal Kishore (2008). A Critical Study of Dalit Literature in India, Online; Accessed on 19 June 2014, Also available at *ULR: http: www. sasnet. lu. se/EASASpapers/4JugalKishore. pdf* (2008): 2.

Mishra, Ram Bali (1989). ***Caste and Caste Conflict.*** Commonwealth Publishers, New Delhi, pp. 1-45.

Mishra, S. N. (2010). Socio-Economic and Political Visions of Dr. B. R. Ambedkar. Concept Publications, New Delhi, pp. 4-33.

Mohanty Manoranjan (2004). Class, Caste and Gender. Sage Publication, New Delhi, pp. 1-154.

Mohindra Vinita and Samina Azhar (2016). Marathi Dalit Literature, Muse India, Online; Accessed on 5 November 2016, Also available at museindia.com regularcontent.asp? issid=40 &id=2976/.

Moretti, Franco (2008). The Novel History and Theory, New Lift Review, Online Accessed on 19 September 2015, Also available at http:/ www.english. ufl.edu/mrg/readin gs/ the%20novel.pdf/.

Murugkar, Lata (1991). Dalit Panthers Movement in Maharashtra: A Sociological Appraisal. Popular Prakashan, Bombay, pp. 1-42.

Nagaraj, D.R. (2010). The Flamming Feet and other essays: The Dalit Movement in India. Permanent Black, New Delhi, pp. 6-47.

Naik, M.K. (1982). A History of Indian English Literature. Sahitya Akademi, New Delhi, pp. 1-55.

Narasimhan, Raji (2012). Dwelling on silence, Online Accessed on 31 December 2016, Also Available at http:// www.thehindu.com/books dwellingonsilence/ article3968311.ece.

Narasimhan, Raji (2011). Meena Kandhaswamy's Touch: The Agression of Suppression, *Language in India*, Vol. 11, No. 5, p. 433.

Narayan, Badri and Misra (2004). Multiple Marginalities: An Anthology of Dalit Writings. Manohar, New Delhi, pp. 1- 45.

Nimbalkar, Waman (2006). Dalit literature: Nature and Role. Prabodhan Prakashan, Nagpur, pp. 1-53.

Nimbalkar, Waman (2009). "Dalit Autobiographies: Graphs of Pain." *Journal of Literature and Aesthetics*, Vol. 9, No. 2, p. 15.

Nimsarkar, P.D. and K. Dasaradhi (2015). Feminism: A Perspective Study, International Journal of English Language, Literature and Humanities *(IJELLH)*, Vol. 3, No. 9, pp. 320-331.

Omvedt, Gail (1994). Dalits and the Democratic revolution: Dr. Ambedkar and the Dalit Movement in Colonial India. Sage Publication, New Delhi, pp. 5-45.

Omvedt, Gail (1995). Dalit Visions. Orient Publications, New Delhi, pp. 1-81.

Omvedt, Gail (2008). Seeking Begumpura. Navayana Publications, New Delhi, pp. 1-55.

Palaka, Prabhakar (2007). Teaching of Dalit Literature in Higher Education Language Forum, Authorsden. Com. Online; Accessed on 23 July 2014, Also available at http://www.authorsden.com/visit/viewArticle.asp?id=47269/.

Pandian, M.S.S. (2007). Brahmin and Non-Brahmin: Genologies of the Tamil Political Present. Permanent Black, New Delhi, pp. 1-42.

Patankar, Bharat and Gail Omvedt (2004). Dalit Liberation Movement in the Colonial Period. Critical Quest, New Delhi, pp. 1-55.

Patel, Neerav (2013). Introduction to the Anthology of Gujarat Dalit Literature, Gujarat Dalit Sahatiya Blogspot, Online; Accessed on 3 December 2014, Also available at http:

gujaratidalitsahitya.blogspot.in/2012/01/ introduction-to anthology-ofgujarati. html.

Patil and Vidhya (2012). Indian English Fiction, Beginning to Modern, *Criterion International Journal in English*, Vol. 3, No.4, pp. 2-8.

Pawar, Urmila and Meenakshi Moon (2008). We also Made History. Trans. Wandana Sonalkar. Zubaan Publications, New Delhi, pp. 1-65.

Prakash, Om (2014). Dalit Literature in India: Some features, *The International Journal of Humanities and Social Studies*, Vol. 2, No. 4, p. 48.

Prasad, Amar Nath (2007). Dalit Literature: A Critical Exploration. Sarup and Sons, New Delhi, pp. 1-65.

Prema Arulselesteen and S. Kalaimani (2016). Double Marginalisation of Dalit women in P. Sivakami's Grip of Change and The Taming of Women, *Criterion International Journal in English*, Vol. 7, No.1, pp. 138-145.

Purushotham, K., Gita Ramaswamy and Gogu Shyamala (2016). The Oxford India Anthology of Telugu Dalit Writing. Oxford University Press, New Delhi, pp. 1-75.

Qureshi, Vaseemahmed (2013). The Search for Self and Space by Indian Dalit Joseph Macwan and African American Richard Wright, *Galaxy: International Multidisciplinary Research Journal*, Vol. 2, No. 5, pp. 2-3.

Rakesh Sheeba (2011). Translating Amrit Lal Nagar's Nachyo Bahut Gopal: Some Considerations—Casteist and Linguistic, The Criterion International Journal in English, Vol. 2, No. 2, pp. 1-14.

Rao, Parimala (2010). Educate Women and Lose Nationality. Critical Quest, New Delhi, pp. 1-41.

Rao, Sudhakara (2016). A Discourse on Caste Clashes among Dalits in Bama's Vanmam Vendetta, Online Accessed on 1 Feburuary 2017, Also Available at puneresearch.com/media/ data/issues/572f17b888ec8.pdf.

Ravikumar (2009). Venomous Touch: Notes on Caste, Culture and Politics. Samya, Kolkata, pp. 1- 287.

Rege, Sharmila *(*2006*)*. Writing Caste/Writing Gender: Narrating Dalit Women's Testimonies. *Zuban,* New Delhi, pp. 1-96.

Sangwan, Om Prakash *(*1996*)*. Dalit Society and the Challenge of Development. Commonwealth Publishers, New Delhi, pp. 1-51.

Sarangi, Jaydeep (2015). Subaltern Speaks: Selected Essays on Sharankumar Limbale. Cyber Net, Allahabad, pp. 1-116.

Sarkar, R.M. (2006). Dalits in India: Past and Present. Serial Publication, New Delhi, pp. 1-378.

Sasidharan, R. (2015). Key Texts in Hindi Dalit Literature: A Thumbnail Analytical Sketch, *Contemporary Research in India*, Vol. 5, No. 2, pp. 142-147.

Satyanarayana and Susie Tharu (2011). No Alphabet Insight: New Dalit writing from South India. Penguin, New Delhi, pp. 1-81.

Satyanarayana and Susie Tharu (2013). Steel Nibs are Sprouting: New Dalit writing from South India. Harper & Collins, Uttar Pradesh, pp. 1-45.

Sehgal, Vikrant (2012). Dalit Literature: A Reading, Literature in English: A Perspective, Online; Accessed on 12 August 2015, Also available at http:/ littcritt.blogspot.in/2012/09/ dalit-literature-reading.html/.

Sen, Samitha (2000). Towards a Feminist Poetics? The Indian Women's Movement AHistorical Perspective, *Policy Research Report on Gender and Development Working Paper Series,* No. 5, pp. 1-70.

Shaw, Ghanshyam (2001). Dalit Identity and Politics. Sare, New Delhi, pp. 155.

Sherrif, K.M. (2016). Intro Dalit Poetry In Malayalam, Scribd, Online; Accessed on 5 November 2016, Also available at https://www.scribd.com doc/30465065/Intro-Dalit- Poetry-in-Malayalam.

Siddique, Farah (2014). Dalit Literature: Issues and Trends, *European ademic research*, Vol. 1, No. 12, pp. 5912-5913.

Simon, Sibhu and Sarojini Sudha (2012). Beautiful Blacks Dignified Dalits. Sarup Book Publishers, New Delhi, pp. 1-55.

Singh, Abinish (2011). A Chronological Study of Indian English Fiction with Social Perspective, *Shodh Sanchayan Bilingual Journal of Humanities and Social Sciences*, Vol. 2, No. 1 and 2, pp. 1-4.

Singh, Sajan and Anjali Srivastava (2016). "Dalit literature in India: An Agitation to a Genre, *International Journal of English Language Literature and Humanities*, Vol. 4, No. 4, pp. 228-234.

Singha, Sankar Prasad and Indranil Acharya (2014). Towards Social Change: Essays on Dalit literature. Orient Black Swan, Hyderabad, pp. 1-45.

Soble, Alan (2002). The Philosophy of Sex- Contemporary Reading. Rowman and Little Field Publishers, United States of America, pp. 5-33.

Somer John (2001). Empowering the Oppressed. Sage Publications, New Delhi, pp. 1-55.

Sreekala, K. (2015). Social consciousness in Dalit Writing, *International Journal of English Language, Literature and Translation Studies* (IJELR), Vol. 2, No. 4. pp. 216-218.

Sundar Syam, Chintha (2015). The Meaning of Dalit and its True Perceptions by Indian Society and Dalit Writers through Translations: An Analytical Study, International Journal on Studies in English Language and Literature (IJSELL), Vol. 3, No. 2, pp. 83-86.

Suresh Adagale Anil (2015). Protest Against Untouchablity in Dalit Poetry, International Journal of English Language, Literature and Translation Studies *(IJELR),* Vol. 2, No. 1, pp. 253-256.

Suryakumari, A. (1993). Women Studies: An Emerging Discipline. Gyan Publishing, New Delhi, pp. 1-53.

Tharakam, Bojja (1994). The First All India Dalit Writers Conference: A Commemorative Volume. Dr B. R. Ambedkar Memorial Trust, Hyderabad, pp.1-33.

Tripathy, Rebati Bhallav (1994). Dalits: A Sub-Human Society. Ashish Publishing House, New Delhi, pp. 1-55.

Trivedi, Pragnesh (2013). Dalit literature: Past and Present, *KGC Journal of Humanity*, Vol. 2, No. 7, p. 1.

Umakant and Sukhadeo Thorat (2004). Caste, Race and Discrimination. Rawat Publications, New Delhi, pp. 1-322.

Victor William, S.L. (2016). Types of novel and which one you should write, Creative writing now, Online; Accessed on 5 May 2016, Also available at http://www.creativewriting-now.com/types-of- novels.html#.

Walters, Margaret (2005). Feminism. Oxford University Press, Oxford, pp. 1-43.

Young and J.C. Robert (2003). Post Colonialism. Oxford University Press, Oxford, pp. 1-33.

Young, Tary (2008). Studying English Literature. Cambridge University Press, New Delhi, pp. 5-55.

Zelliot Eleanor and Deo Veena (1994). Dalit Literature twenty Five Years of Protest or Progress, *Journal of South Asian Literature*, Vol. 29, No. 2, pp. 41-67.

Zelliot Eleanor and Mulk Raj Anand (1992). An Anthology of Dalit Literature (Poems). Gyan Publishing House, New Delhi, pp. 1- 65.

Zelliot Eleanor (1992). From Untouchable to Dalit: Essays on the Ambedkar Movement. Manohar, New Delhi, pp. 1-54.

Zelliot Eleanor (1998). Essays on Ambedkar Movement. Manohar, New Delhi, pp. 1-45.

Index

B

L

N

R

S